The Perennial Philosophy

Series

World Wisdom
The Library of Perennial Philosophy

The Library of Perennial Philosophy is dedicated to the exposition of the timeless Truth underlying the diverse religions. This Truth, often referred to as the *Sophia Perennis*—or Perennial Wisdom—finds its expression in the revealed Scriptures as well as the writings of the great sages and the artistic creations of the traditional worlds.

God and Work: Aspects of Art and Tradition appears as one of our selections in the Perennial Philosophy series.

The Perennial Philosophy Series

In the beginning of the twentieth century, a school of thought arose which has focused on the enunciation and explanation of the Perennial Philosophy. Deeply rooted in the sense of the sacred, the writings of its leading exponents establish an indispensable foundation for understanding the timeless Truth and spiritual practices which live in the heart of all religions. Some of these titles are companion volumes to the Treasures of the World's Religions series, which allows a comparison of the writings of the great sages of the past with the perennialist authors of our time.

Cover: "God as the Architect of the Universe", miniature
from a French *Bible moralisée*, mid 13th century

GOD AND WORK

Aspects of Art and Tradition

BRIAN KEEBLE

Foreword by

Wendell Berry

World Wisdom

God and Work: Aspects of Art and Tradition
© 2009 World Wisdom, Inc.

Library of Congress Cataloging-in-Publication Data

Keeble, Brian.
  God and work : aspects of art and tradition / Brian Keeble ; foreword
by Wendell Berry.
      p. cm. -- (The perennial philosophy series)
Includes bibliographical references and index.
   ISBN 978-1-933316-68-0 (pbk. : alk. paper) 1. Work--Religious
aspects. 2. Art--Religious aspects. 3. Art--Philosophy. I. Title.
  BL65.W67K44 2009
  204--dc22

                                                           2009006550

Printed on acid-free paper in The United States of America.

For information address World Wisdom, Inc.
P.O. Box 2682, Bloomington, Indiana 47402-2682
www.worldwisdom.com

CONTENTS

Foreword by Wendell Berry .... *ix*

Preface .... *xi*

1. A. K. Coomaraswamy and the True Art of Living 1
2. W. R. Lethaby on Art and Labor 15
3. Archetype as Letterform: The "Dream" of Edward
   Johnston 29
4. Eric Gill: Towards a Holy Tradition of Work 41
5. Of Art and Skill 63
6. Thoughts on Reading Frithjof Schuon's Writings on Art ... 75
7. William Blake: Art as Divine Vision 85

Afterword 99
Selected Bibliography 105
Biographical Notes 109
Index 111

[The] integration of work into spirituality depends on three fundamental conditions which we shall designate respectively by the terms "necessity", "sanctification" and "perfection". The first of these conditions implies that the activity to be spiritualized correspond to a necessity and not to a mere whim: one can sanctify — namely offer to God—any normal activity necessitated by the requirements of life itself, but not just any occupation lacking a sufficient reason or having a reprehensible character; this amounts to saying that any necessary activity possesses a character that predisposes it to conveying the spirit; all necessary activities in fact have a certain universality which renders them eminently symbolic.

The second of the three conditions implies that the activity thus defined be actually offered to God, which is to say that it be done through love of God and without rebelling against destiny; this is the meaning of the prayers by which—in most if not all traditional forms—work is consecrated, and thus ritualized, meaning that it becomes a "natural sacrament", a kind of shadow or secondary counterpart of the "supernatural sacrament" that is the rite properly speaking.

Finally, the third condition implies the logical perfection of the work, for it is evident that one cannot offer an imperfect thing to God, nor consecrate a base object to Him; moreover, the perfection of the act is as self-evident as that of existence itself, in the sense that every act is supposed to retrace the Divine Act and at the same time a modality of it. This perfection of action comprises three aspects, which refer respectively to the activity as such, then to the means, and finally to the purpose; in other words, the activity as such has to be objectively and subjectively perfect, which implies that it be conformable or proportionate to the end to be attained; the means should also be conformable and proportionate to the goal envisioned, which implies that the instrument of the work be well chosen, then wielded with skill, which is to say in perfect conformity with the nature of the work; finally, the result of the work has to be perfect, and must answer exactly to the need from which it has arisen.

Frithjof Schuon

The night cometh, when no man can work.

John 9:4

FOREWORD

That we are living through a time of disintegration is a fact by now merely obvious to anybody who is paying attention. T. S. Eliot famously described this disintegration as a "dissociation of sensibility"—a radical disconnection between thinking and feeling, mind and heart. William Butler Yeats noted simply that "Things fall apart". William Carlos Williams thought the modern age was characterized by "divorce". He meant the coming apart, not just of marriage, but of all other things that ought to hold together and that might be held together by a vital language and art, a local imagination rising from the ground underfoot. Ananda Coomaraswamy, one of the subjects of the present book, addressed precisely Mr. Keeble's concern by speaking of the divorce of usefulness and beauty, which certainly involves the divorce of work and pleasure. Eric Gill, another of Mr. Keeble's subjects, wrote of the divorce between industrial workers and any knowledge of what they are making, let alone any responsibility for its use or quality.

And so by a necessity plain enough, this is a book about work. If things are falling apart, how are they to be put together again? Well, only by human work. But this must be work of a certain quality and kind. The artists and critics who are the subjects of this book are people who have undertaken to restore the integrity of humans individually and of human communities and cultures. They have undertaken to do this by re-including in our consciousness and conscience all that has been excluded both by the materialism of the "developed" world and by the exclusive religiosity of the dominant forms of religion.

Materialism, you might think, would follow a logic of respect for material reality. But instead, by a seeming paradox, materialism holds all materials in contempt and it is destroying the world. Its typical results are pollution, soil erosion, and the destruction of the cultures of husbandry and caretaking. Or you might think that religion would hold in reverence the creation of the Creator. But religion long ago ceded to the materialists all responsibility for the economy and technology of our worldly life. This is the result of yet another modern divorce: the life of the body is to be determined by the industrial corporations, their academic apologists, and their political defenders, whereas the life of the soul will be the business of religion. The soul is directed Heavenward while work and the world go to Hell.

The bad results of our disintegration are thus perfectly integrated: our world and our souls are equally and similarly diseased. Clearly something more, something else, is needed. Clearly, the work of re-integration has to be at once thoughtful and practical, economic and beautiful. I think this book puts us on the right path, which is not surprising for it is written by exactly the right author. For many years, as a book designer and publisher, Brian Keeble has practiced, exemplified, and served the kind of work and the principles that he defends in these essays. Nobody better understands the difference between "information" and "communication"—disorderly, ugly, produced for captives and addicts—and books well-written, well-designed, and well-made.

By putting "God" and "work" in the same title—in, so to speak, the same breath—Mr. Keeble challenges the modern orthodoxy, which has done its best to keep those terms separate. The great dissociation of which T. S. Eliot and others have spoken has made it likely that people will exclude from their forms of worship any reference to their economic life or the quality of their work, and that they will exclude from their work any sense of religious obligation.

By bringing those two words back into their old association, and by the honor he gives to people who conscientiously kept them associated, Mr. Keeble restores to practical viability the idea of good work. He brings again into view the possibility of religion practicable in work, and work compatible with worship and wholly meant.

Wendell Berry
Lanes Landing Farm
Port Royal, Kentucky

PREFACE

The words "God" and "work" are seldom closely associated in the modern mind. The former denotes something remote from daily affairs, even unlikely and outmoded for a significant number of people, now that the evolutionary hypothesis has been absorbed into so many areas of thought. Work, on the other hand, concerns only what comes to hand in the expenditure of time and effort required to secure a livelihood. Is this division healthy? Is it inevitable? We spend the best part of our lives at work. Are we to conclude that during all those hours of using our mental and physical faculties there is no reason to connect our effort with possible answers to those persistent questions we have concerning our identity, place, and purpose in the world? We know that such questions will not go away by being ignored. And we often find ourselves unable to escape the conclusion that work is somehow intimately bound up with whatever we think the deeper meaning of life might be, even if making such connections does not take an overtly religious form.

So, to bring together God and work as mutually present and effective realities, we need a bridge: a bridge that allows us to explore the possible continuities between our deepest intuitions about the meaning of life and the more worldly business that is the accomplishment of work. Clearly this is no simple task. Nor is it a task so far unstarted, as I hope the following studies will show. And we should not shrink from the task—through work, prayer, and contemplation—because it seems everything might be a lost cause on the one hand, and on the other because the task looks likely to incline us to admit that the work-a-day world we now accept as normal is urgently in need of realignment if it is ever to harness the truth, beauty, and goodness that are at the root of our deepest intuitions. That is to say, even if we conclude that the modern world is so constituted as to unnaturally force apart what ought otherwise to be a natural attachment between our earthly vocation and what it means to be human. Undoubtedly, what the modern industrial and now increasingly post-industrial world offers, in this respect, amounts to our being condemned, during most of our working hours at least, to activities that have no bearing on our final destiny. No doubt, too, this division is yet one more outcome of the fragmentation that characterizes the modern mentality that no longer recognizes a noumenal order of reality (and its organ of perception, metaphysical intuition), which alone can unify natural things with spiritual things.

Traditionally—if such a contraction be allowed—any form of intellectual aim that did not take account of this antecedent, archetypal order of reality would have been considered all but invalid. Now, in many quarters, to give any sort of credence to its effective presence is likely to be seen as a sign of willful eccentricity. Such problems, however, are not the direct concern of the following studies, though it is as well to be aware of this ultimate cause.

What if we ask, has this division between God and work always existed? Or can we look to a civilization and a culture where, what must by any measure be regarded as major dimensions of life and thought, such a radical divide was by no means the norm? In other words, are there periods of history for which work, vocation, and spirituality were mutually supportive aspects of life: and that resulting in a culture whose artefacts, from cities to the implements of everyday life, touch upon depths of meaning and beauty that are inconceivable from the perspective of our experience of what is required to sustain a livelihood?

Of course, such questions have been answered, and answered in the affirmative both in the context of practicing a craft (as with, for instance, Eric Gill and Edward Johnston), as well as in the context of a comprehensively scholarly approach. In the latter case the name of A. K. Coomaraswamy stands supreme in virtue of the range and penetration of his writings. All these studies presume upon the work of Coomaraswamy though not upon the reader's familiarity with it.

At the core of Coomaraswamy's work is the idea of a primordial metaphysic common to the world's religions. This body of doctrine, symbolism, and spiritual method (each integral to the religion in question), at one and the same time applies to the substance of spiritual realization as to the immediate factors that comprise human vocation. This body of traditional wisdom has come to be known as the *sophia* or *religio perennis*, in order to distinguish it from the merely horizontal process that is the cumulative effect of historical continuity. This distinction is important. The *religio perennis* is not the property of a past culture or of a specific set of selected, ideal, cultural circumstances. Were that to be the case then any appeal to it as a form of wisdom that might illuminate the penumbra that is the ending of a civilization (such as we inhabit) would be fruitless, and likely end in yet another superstructure of human arrogance and invention such as is all too familiar. Providence dictates that we deal with the problems that directly face us now. The subjects of the following studies, all, in their different ways, and according to the varying demands of their respective vocations, appeal to the traditional wisdom as a means of coming to terms with what they perceive to be an impoverishment in the modern world. This impoverishment is nothing less than a depletion of the proper content and practice of life. Each of our subjects has made, as I hope becomes evident, a significant contribution to the never-ending task of determining what it means to be human and thence to what this meaning obliges us to undertake if we are to attempt a union of the contemplative and active life. In singling out the work of Coomaraswamy I am merely signaling a particular indebtedness of my own, as well as, in some cases, an indebtedness of several of the subjects themselves.

It is my hope and intention that these studies, while remaining aware of the necessary, impending darkness announced by our second epigraph, may make some contribution to the healing of that division between God and work, a process we ignore at the cost of putting all aspects of our culture in jeopardy. In this respect the present collection might be considered as a companion to an earlier one: *Art: For Whom and For What?*[1]

The chapters on W. R. Lethaby and Edward Johnston were originally commissioned by and given as papers to the Edward Johnston Foundation's Ditchling International Seminars of 2003 and 2004.

---

[1] Brian Keeble, *Art: For Whom and For What?* (Ipswich: Golgonooza Press, 1998).

They were subsequently published, along with the chapter on A. K. Coomaraswamy in *On the Nature and Significance of the Crafts*, published by Temenos Academy, London, 2005. The chapter on Eric Gill is a slightly revised version of the Introduction to *A Holy Tradition of Working: Passages from the Writings of Eric Gill*, Ipswich, UK, 1983. "William Blake: Art as Divine Vision" was first delivered as a lecture at the Temenos Academy, London, in 2004 and was subsequently published in *Temenos Academy Review*, 9, 2004. "Thoughts on Reading Frithjof Schuon's Writings on Art" first appeared in *Sophia*, volume 4, no. 7, 1998. "Of Art of Skill" was first published in *Sacred Web*, volume 17, 2006.

I am indebted to John Carey, Stephen Overy, and Jill Burrows for their help in preparing the final texts. It is a pleasure to record my gratitude to Stephen Williams and Susana Marin of World Wisdom for their enthusiastic collaboration. Finally, and not for the first time, I am indebted to Wendell Berry for his finding time to contribute a Foreword to this book.

Brian Keeble
August 2008

1

A. K. Coomaraswamy
and the True Art of Living

In our Preface (and, indeed, elsewhere) reference is made to the work of A. K. Coomaraswamy as if he were a benchmark, an exemplar, when it comes to understanding the deeper issues concerning matters of art, craft, work, and the human vocation. These references were quite deliberate and they are not the first to regard Coomaraswamy in this way. In his *Autobiography*, Eric Gill eulogized Coomaraswamy and thought his exposition of what Coomaraswamy himself called "the traditional philosophy of art" was quite simply the truth of the matter.[1] This is no small claim; and others have written in similar vein. The time has come, then, to examine what this claim rests upon.

Ananda Kentish Coomaraswamy was born in 1877 in Colombo, Ceylon (as it was then) of a distinguished Ceylonese father and an English mother. He grew up and was educated in England, entering University College, London, in 1897, and receiving a B.Sc. in Geology and Botany, with First Class Honors, in 1900. In 1906 he earned his doctorate (D.Sc.) with a thesis largely on the mineralogy of Ceylon. He was the first Ceylonese

---

[1] "There was one person, to whom I think William Rothenstein introduced me, whom I might not have met otherwise and to whose influence I am deeply grateful; I mean the philosopher and theologian, Ananda Coomaraswamy. Others have written the truth about life and religion and man's work. Others have written good clear English. Others have had the gift of witty exposition. Others have understood the metaphysics of Christianity and others have understood the metaphysics of Hinduism and Buddhism. Others have understood the true significance of erotic drawings and sculptures. Others have seen the relationships of the true and the good and the beautiful. Others have had apparently unlimited learning. Others have loved; others have been kind and generous. But I know of no one else in whom all these gifts and all these powers have been combined. I dare not confess myself his disciple; that would only embarrass him. I can only say that I believe that no other living writer has written the truth in matters of art and life and religion and piety with such wisdom and understanding" (Eric Gill, *Autobiography* [London: Jonathan Cape, 1940], p. 174).

to earn London University's highest degree. It is worth noting that this early scientific training stayed with him throughout his life, "coloring" the presentation of his scholarly findings with objectivity and precision.

In the early years of the twentieth century he undertook several field trips in Ceylon (in 1904 he discovered a new mineral there, which he named thorianite), and it was during one of these trips that he had an experience that was the awakening moment of the rest of his life's work. Seeing a Sinhalese mother and child wearing bedraggled and filthy western clothes, not without some pride, made him reflect on how western commercialism was, the world over, destroying the inner spirit of the way of life of traditional societies. This was, of course, at a time when the mercantile British Empire was at its height, its commercialism having "conquered" much of the world. But we must also take into account the fact that Coomaraswamy grew up in an England which was, after Ruskin and Morris, offering both an intellectual and a practical challenge to the hegemony of industrialism.

These challenges Coomaraswamy was familiar with when he came to write his first book, *Mediaeval Sinhalese Art*.[2] In the Foreword to this survey of the, then, remnants of the indigenous arts and crafts of Ceylon, he not only gives a brief summary of arguments against the encroaching barbarism of the industrial juggernaut, but also sketches the outlines of the territory which his thinking was to encompass over the next three decades. Here, he did not shy away from announcing to the world that he would henceforth concern himself with "the true Art of Living which has for so long been neglected by humanity". And so he did. As with Ruskin, Morris, and others before him, the germ of his ideas seems to have been located in an indignation at the cultural depreciation and social injustice which afflict modern society as a consequence of the divorce of art from labor. This, he was bound to admit, was a catastrophe both for society and any culture worthy of the name. With such contemporaries as C. R. Ashbee, A. J. Penty, and W. R. Lethaby, Coomaraswamy could acknowledge that machines had come to stay, so that he was simply of his age in asking by what

---

[2] Broad Campden: Essex House Press, 1908.

means they might be controlled: how could "a curse" be transformed into "a blessing". For, as he suggested in his Introduction, "a community cannot afford to dispense with the intellectual and imaginative forces, the educational and ethical factors which go with the existence of skilled craftsmen and small workshops". The divorce of art from labor has an outcome injurious to both. From the point of view of the worker, "through the division of labor [he is] no longer able to make any whole thing [but is] confined to making small parts of things. . . . He can never [thereby] rise in virtue of his knowledge or experience in the craft itself. That craft is for him destroyed as a means of culture,[3] and the community has lost one more man's intelligence".

From the point of view of the artist divorced from labor, imagination, which ought to be united with appropriate technique, is severed from a qualifying formality, and so is "free" to create the fantasies and unrealities that are the expression of subjective "moods" and "feelings". This is nothing less than to make "the sufficient aim of art . . . the giving of pleasure. This reduction of the highest aim of art from prophecy to amusement strikes at the root of any possible revival of true art."

These were the themes that occupied Coomaraswamy at the start of his prodigious, scholarly career.[4] Yet they were, for the most part, received ideas; the staple of much of the thinking of the Arts and Crafts dissenters to which Coomaraswamy was, at this stage, signing up. What was to take him much deeper than his forebears was his steady, persistent concentration on, and scholarly documentation of, the principles of the *normal*, or traditional philosophy of art. Coomaraswamy had no personal philosophy to espouse; what was unique was the manner of his profound exposi-

---

[3] The word "culture" is one the mind slips over all too easily in an age when it has come to mean not much more than simply "what people do". Coomaraswamy has in mind the older, semantic ties of the word with "cult", "cultivate", from the Latin *colere*, to till. It is through treading the path, or trade, of his own vocation that a man cultivates the "soil" of his inherently spiritual nature.

[4] For a discussion of the wider nature of Coomaraswamy's scholarly researches see the author's essay "A. K. Coomaraswamy: Scholar of the Spirit", in *The Essential Sophia*, edited by Seyyed Hossein Nasr and Katherine O'Brien (Bloomington, IN: World Wisdom, 2006), pp. 274-87.

tion of a universal doctrine of human identity, vocation, art, craft, and work grounded in the understanding that the whole purpose of life is the realization of an inner, essential, spiritual Self. What the body of Coomaraswamy's writings offers is an understanding of the place and significance of the crafts in human society that lifts it far beyond any discussion of the relative merits of techniques of production, any judgment as to the fruits of labor or any weighing of the justice of its material rewards. Coomaraswamy embeds his vision of the crafts within the matrix of a whole wisdom about the fulfillment of the active life of making and doing seen in relation to the vocation and final destiny of man. The wisdom in question encompasses, at one end, matters pertaining to the interaction of mind, eye, and hand, and moves through the various doctrines that articulate the distinction of art from prudence, with its cognate teaching that distinguishes artistic sin from moral sin, the doctrine of art as a habit of intellect as opposed to aesthetic category, the theory of beauty as a property of the cognitive faculty; to the symbolism of craft procedures and indeed of all things as the transformative substance of spiritual regeneration. At its highest, this wisdom arrives at an understanding of how the human maker may act analogously to the Divine Creator, echoing the "art" of God's creating the phenomenal world from noumenal levels of reality in as much as he, the craftsman, makes from some already existing substance what does not yet exist in nature. He thus is said to "imitate nature in her manner of operation", in the words of St. Thomas that Coomaraswamy so frequently quotes. How, then, does this process of imitation work?

The central premise of Coomaraswamy's scholarly synthesis is the idea that all religions have a common metaphysical basis. Indeed, he thought of the religions as being the various dialects of a universal language of the Spirit. Notwithstanding that each religion possesses a body of doctrine, a cosmology, and an integral symbolism proper to itself, each speaks the language of an ultimate Reality that is common to all. This explains how, in his scholarly presentation, Coomaraswamy could move effortlessly from one tradition to another, quoting scriptures, sacred texts, works of ancient wisdom, manuals of spiritual and practical instruction, in order to reveal a doctrine of art that is universally true. He thought of this doctrine as being part of a *sophia perennis*, a wisdom about life that with adequate presentation might be rejected but could not be refuted. Each religion, in a way that is integral to it, conceives of the human as created in imitation of the Divine Reality. The words of Genesis (1:27), "So God created man in his own image", are of course familiar. This is but a single formulation of a principial relationship whose implications allow it to be re-cast to state: the Divine becomes man in order that the vocation of man be to seek the Divine Reality. This is the quintessential orientation that underlies the reality of human vocation. Coomaraswamy, in typical fashion, juxtaposes two expressions of this doctrine in his essay "The Philosophy of Mediaeval and Oriental Art" (1938), one from the East and one from the West: "It is by intense devotion to his own vocation that Everyman attains his own perfection" (*Bhagavad Gītā* 18:45), and "the artificer 'co-operates with the will of God when by the use of his body and by his daily care and operation he gives to anything a figure that he shapes in accordance with the divine intent'" (Hermes, *Asclepius* 1:11). All human needs ought to be set within the context of this fundamental orientation and purpose. But this "perfection" has need itself of a means by which it might, through Grace, be effected, for in addition to proposing an analogy between divine creation and human creation, it also implies the means to overcome an intrinsic impediment. To account for this we must recognize that there are "two in us", two "selves": one inner and one outer, that can act in harmony only when the former has governance over the latter, for all our actions of making and doing must either aid or hinder the attainment of our "perfection". Hence the importance of art, for it is by art that our physical needs are brought into alignment with our spiritual needs. By the things of art, works *of* art, we are both inwardly and outwardly nourished.

> Works of art, regarded as food. . . , can only be thought of as "luxuries" when the patron's appetites . . . are excessive. . . ; man eats to live, and can only be thought of as "greedy" . . . when he lives to eat. By works of art the self is nourished in its

vegetative . . . modes of being, and re-minded in its intellectual . . . modes of being; for in every work of art there is a combination of formal-intelligible . . . and material-sensible . . . factors, the former corresponding to the "ear" as symbol of angelic understanding, the latter to the "eye" as symbol of sensational experience.

That is how Coomaraswamy spoke of it in 1937 in his essay "Art in Indian Life".

In his very last essay, "Athena and Hephaistos" (1947), Coomaraswamy elaborates with characteristic penetration and concision on how these two modes of being must be understood: at one extreme are their ultimate symbolic referents, the two deities Athena, the Goddess of Wisdom, and Hephaistos, the Titan smith, both "born of the same father, Zeus"—that is, both, in their individual function, directly reflecting the divine intellect. At the other extreme, they serve to characterize and distinguish the fruitful union of the two faculties of imaginative inspiration and productive technique—that is the operation of art.

> In the production of anything made by art, or the exercise of any art, two faculties, respectively imaginative and operative, free and servile, are simultaneously involved: the former consisting in the conception of some idea in an imitable form, the latter in the imitation (*mimesis*) of this invisible model (*paradeigma*) in some material, which is thus informed. Imitation, the distinctive character of all the arts, is accordingly two-fold, on the one hand the work of intellect (*nous*) and on the other of the hands (*cheir*). These two aspects of the creative activity correspond to the "two in us", viz. our spiritual or intellectual Self and sensitive psycho-physical Ego, working together (*synergoi*). The integration of the work of art will depend upon the extent to which the Ego is able and willing to serve the Self, or if the patron and the workman are two different persons,[5] upon the measure of their mutual understanding.

---

[5] Obviously art is impossible without patronage, albeit the artist may be, on occasion, the patron also—even the consumer. But each of these roles is clearly defined and their respective responsibilities apportioned, as well as the judgment which each incurs. "It is the business of the artist to *know how things ought to*

We need to be aware that behind such expressions as the "exercise" or "operation" of any art there lies in Coomaraswamy's writings a whole body of wisdom and doctrine that is in stark contrast to what is usually evoked today by the words "art" and "artist".

According to the "traditional" philosophy of art that Coomaraswamy traces, all art is a kind of knowledge that begins in God, who creates all things existent from the *nothing* (no-thing, so called), that is, the ineffable reason of divine ideas of things prior to their expression in the phenomenal world. God, who has, as it were, only to "think" for a thing to "be", is imitated by the artificer's intellectual operation whereby he conceives in his imagination the essential form or idea of a thing which he must make prior to the actual execution of it. This act of imagination is the formal cause of the work and the actual execution is said to be the efficient cause of the thing made. This whole process is a "habit"—something like what we might think of as an instinct—of the intellect. It is the cognitive and informing energy of a knowledge of how things are to be made good of their kind. As an intellectual operation it is the norm of workmanship and serves to bind together the maker's interior being with his exterior experience in a "polar balance of metaphysical with physical", as Coomaraswamy puts it. That is to say, the specific wisdom that is art implies an accompanying and appropriate method for its realization. In addition, reason must be capable of guiding and correcting the physical act of making, and for this to be faithfully achieved the "free" exercise of imagination must be anchored in the "fixed" procedures of a servile technique that, so to say, steers the maker's *intention* towards its goal.

We cannot overlook the fact that, in this universal teaching on the location and operation of art *within* the artificer, which was recovered and presented by Coomaraswamy, we are invited to understand how, in the daily activity of making things to serve real needs (as opposed to appeasing appetites), the reciprocal process

be made and to be able accordingly, as it is the business of the patron to know *what things ought to be made,* and of the consumer to know what things *have been well and truly made* and to be able to use them after their kind" ("Art in Indian Life").

that is the integration of the two selves or faculties is bound to induce in the craftsman a heightened degree of spiritual aware-ness, both towards his own nature and towards the "intractable" matter that his art must transform.

Contrariwise, in the sentient drudgery of the industrial worker, the division of whose labor "no longer [renders him] able to make any whole thing, [only] small parts of things", the two faculties are of necessity split apart. For him method is predetermined, and can hardly be an imitation of an intelligible pattern held freely in the imagination. His labor is literally art-less, a matter of mere daily experience, a practice and physical effort from which most of the elements of real and responsible judgment, assessment, and correction have been removed. Not for him the conception of a good and wise production entertained and then executed accord-ingly by the integration of mind, eye, and hand. Not for him the experience of work as a support for contemplation, the realization that work is prayer: for the industrial (and post-industrial) worker matters of the spirit, of contemplation, of prayer, of art, and work inhabit discrete worlds. Not for him the possibility that, in making something, he loves it into existence in the manner in which it can be said that God loved the world into existence.

However, it is not the machine *per se* that is to blame for such a state of affairs, so much as the fact that in the division of labor the imaginative function is denied. In his essay "A Figure of Speech or a Figure of Thought" (1946), Coomaraswamy explained the exact nature of the diminishment effected by this denial:

> an act of "imagination" in which the idea to be represented is first clothed in the imitable form or image of the thing to be made, must precede the operation in which this form is impressed upon the actual material. The first of these acts . . . is free, the second servile. It is only if the first be omitted that the word "servile" acquires a dishonorable connotation; then we can speak only of labor, and not of art. It need hardly be argued that our methods of manufacture are, in this shameful sense, servile, nor be denied that the industrial system, for which these methods are needed, is an abomination "unfit for free men". A system of manufacture governed by money values presupposes that there shall be two different kinds of makers, privileged artists who may be "inspired", and underprivileged laborers,

unimaginative by hypothesis, since they are required only to make what other men have imagined, or more often only to copy what other men have already made. It has often been claimed that the productions of "fine" art are useless; it would seem to be a mockery to speak of a society as "free" where it is only the makers of useless things who are supposedly free.

And in his essay "Introduction to the Art of Eastern Asia" (1932), Coomaraswamy gives a further elaboration of this diminishment in so far as machine facture has led to the divorce of beauty and utility:

During the greater part of the world's history, every product of human workmanship, whether icon, platter, or shirt button, has been at once beautiful and useful. This normal condition has persisted longer in Asia than anywhere else. If it no longer exists in Europe and America, this is by no means the fault of invention or machinery as such: man has always been an inventive and tool- or machine-using creature. The art of the potter was not destroyed by the potter's wheel. How far from reasonable it would be to attribute the present abnormal condition to a baneful influence exerted on man by science and machinery is demonstrated in the fact that beauty and use are now only found together in the work of engineers—in bridges, airplanes, dynamos, and surgical instruments, the forms of which are governed by scientific principles and absolute functional necessity. If beauty and use are not now generally seen together in household utensils and businessmen's costumes, nor generally in factory-made objects, this is not the fault of the machinery employed, but incidental to our lowered conception of human dignity, and consequent insensibility to real values. The exact measure of our indifference to these values is reflected in the current distinction of fine and decorative art, it being required that the first shall have no use, the second no meaning: and in our equivalent distinction of the inspired artist or genius from the trained workman. We have convinced ourselves that art is a thing too good for this world, labor too brutal an activity to be mentioned in the same breath with art; that the artist is one not much less than a prophet, the workman not much more than an animal. Thus a perverted idealism and an amazing insensibility exist side by side; neither condition could, in fact, exist without the other.

According to the traditional philosophy of art, there is no essential difference in kind between artist, craftsman, artificer, or workman. They are all one and the same and are differentiated only in terms that allow discussion of their respective practical functions. Art is a skill appropriate to every specific operation that is the making or arranging of something and remains with the maker. Art is a "habit" of mind applied to a set of practical circumstances, which presupposes that a perfection of work is to be attained. Art, as Coomaraswamy never tired of pointing out, stays *in* the artist.

This view contrasts sharply with the view of the modern world, where art is—albeit somewhat vaguely—understood as something exercised for its own sake, which exercise produces objects imbued with the aesthetic and emotional idiosyncrasies of their creators.[6] These *things* are themselves called "art" and are thought of categorically as being specially set apart from the objects of utility that we need in order to live. According to the modern acceptance of the term, the artist is a special kind of person, whereas for the traditional philosophy every person is a special kind of artist. The modern view assumes that some sort of aesthetic pleasure is the purpose of art, whereas the traditional philosophy holds that, though we may take pleasure in perfecting the operation by which a well and truly made thing is made, none the less pleasure "is not a need in us independent of our need for the things themselves". Such pleasure is part of our nature, but it is not the goal or specific purpose of art.

From what has been said so far it might be inferred that the traditional philosophy envisages that a culture of craft-making would of itself make for a near-perfect society. Any such inference would be a mistake. There are many things beside art that must go to make up a good society. The traditional philosophy makes a clear distinction between the particular end of art, which is the

[6] See chapter 5, "Of Art and Skill".

good of the thing to be made, and the general end of art which is the good of man. Which is to say that there will be actions taken with a view to the good of life itself but which are not art—acts of charity, for instance. This amounts to a distinction between the moral imperatives of action and the good intention of making; between the good that is the end of our behavior in general and the good that is the end of skilled action in particular. It is also a distinction that guards against the glorification of work for its own sake. Coomaraswamy frequently illustrates this distinction with reference to Aristotle's *Nicomachean Ethics*, according to which "Prudence is the norm of conduct. . . . Art is the norm of work-manship". The artificer possesses his art, *as maker,* for the good of the work to be done, not specifically for the good of his person. However, the good in either case implies the possibility of sin, in the sense of "a departure from the order to the end". A craftsman may sin morally and artistically, being guilty as a man in the first instance and as an artist in the second. In his essay "The Mediaeval Theory of Beauty" (1935), Coomaraswamy uses the analogy of the smith, who "will be sinning as an artist if he fails to make a sharp knife, but as a man if he makes one in order to commit murder, or for someone whom he *knows* to intend to commit murder".

Such distinctions may seem without relevance to the average modern workman, who does not expect his daily "job" to have any bearing on the destiny of his soul. But the universality of the doctrine that distinguishes art and morals, as Coomaraswamy demonstrates it, makes it more than obvious that the reciprocity between a man's vocation as an artificer and his ultimate destiny was traditionally played out by men and women going about the tasks that provide for their daily needs, spiritual and material at once. Here there are no separate compartments for material needs, aesthetic feelings, and spiritual nourishment. It emerges that the artist/craftsman, in order to be able to "rise in virtue of his knowl-edge or experience in the craft itself" (to return to the words of the Foreword to *Mediaeval Sinhalese Art*) must be free to address himself, through the act of making, to something over and above the exertion of his skill: for skill is, by definition, applied to some-thing other than itself, as meaning is always inherent and beyond expression.

Coomaraswamy wrote no specific paper devoted to the question of machine facture and its consequences. His writings nevertheless contain, sometimes in the body of the text, more often in a lengthy footnote, unequivocal censure of the effects of the industrial way of life in so far as it was detrimental to what the worker might get *by* working, rather than what he might hope to get *from* his work. Coomaraswamy did not live to see the further consequence of industrialism: its fatal impact on the natural world.

If the process of making things is judged only in the light of quantitative factors then of course the machine product will be preferred to the relatively "primitive" production methods we associate with the crafts. But that is hardly the point. There is nothing in the process of machine production to determine the criteria of *need* by which we decide what is necessary as opposed to what is merely expedient production for economic gain. We forget that technological innovation only gains acceptance as a result of complex, often subliminal powers of persuasion.[7] We live in a dual world, an order of reality whose fabric is woven of things that can be co-defined by their opposite: Creator/creation; life/death; masculine/feminine; good/evil; beauty/ugliness; active/passive; inner/outer. It is impossible to conceive of one of these complementary pairs without its opposite being implied. Each is meaningless without the other. Nothing can enter this order of reality with, so to say, a single face. Nothing can be an absolute good—a good without qualification—in the order of relativity. The knife that so perfectly serves to cut can be the instrument of murder, as Coomaraswamy pointed out. The nuclear power that provides such an abundance of energy comes at the price—incalculable—of disposing of its toxic waste. The medicine that cures

[7] To deride anti-industrialism, on the grounds of its failure to acknowledge the natural and inevitable course of events that is the progress of technology, in turn fails to grasp that there is nothing "inevitable" about the subjection of men to their own inventions, however it may be understandable. The "optical illusion" of this seeming inevitability has received detailed examination by Jacques Ellul in *The Technological Bluff* (Grand Rapids, MI: Eerdmans, 1960), in which he demonstrates how an earlier acquiescence in the face of industrial manufacture has now been replaced by a subservience to the propaganda of technologies.

or alleviates illness and disease is produced as part and parcel of the science of chemical production that also pollutes.

There can be little doubt that Coomaraswamy thought that his scholarly synthesis was the expression of a true philosophy of life. He presents his findings with an uncompromising rigor which suggests that he might at least have entertained the idea that the traditional philosophy would only have to be witnessed to be believed and in some measure realized, if only by the sheer persuasive force of Truth itself. His work certainly makes no concession to human sentimentality. But in a world that is imperfect, what would be the point of aiming at anything less than perfection?

2

W. R. Lethaby on Art and Labor

Priscilla Johnston said of her father Edward Johnston that "only one man influenced him profoundly and for life, William Richard Lethaby". She relates how, within hours of arriving in London on the night train from Edinburgh on 4 April 1898, her father was taken by Harry Cowlishaw to Gray's Inn Square and introduced to Lethaby. Reflecting on the significance of this meeting with the founder of the then fledgling Central School of Arts and Crafts, Johnston thought of it as "the miracle of my life". Many years later, with an eye to what this meeting had done to shape his life, Johnston concluded, "I think it nothing less than a Divine Providence".

Some forty years after meeting him, Eric Gill said of Lethaby, "who shall measure the greatness of this man—one of the few men of the nineteenth century whose minds were enlightened directly by the Holy Spirit".

It was Lethaby who, on seeing some of Johnston's "parchments" (his early attempts at calligraphy), sent the younger man off to the British Museum in search of good letterform models in early manuscripts, and promptly put Johnston in charge of a class in calligraphy which he was planning to start at the Central School. It was Lethaby who commissioned Johnston's *Writing and Illuminating, and Lettering*. Moreover, it was Lethaby who suggested to Gill—who was in Johnston's first class—that he take up stonemasonry and who bequeathed to him, as to many others, the notion of "art-nonsense".

These few facts alone, if one thinks of the legacy of Johnston and Gill, ought to prompt us to ask what sort of ideas motivated this exceptional man. I will make no attempt to give a comprehensive portrait of Lethaby the man and of the full range of his interests, but will concentrate mainly on the core of his ideas to do with art, labor, the crafts, and the impact that these have on society at large.

William Richard Lethaby was born in Barnstaple, Devon, in 1857. As a young man he trained as an architect, moving to London in 1879 where, at the age of twenty-two, he began work as Chief Clerk to Norman Shaw. During the next decade Lethaby gained a position in the thriving Arts and Crafts milieu that had been established on the basis of the precepts and practice of Ruskin and Morris.

In a short essay on Ruskin which he wrote in 1919 Lethaby listed, off the top of his head, what lessons he had absorbed from Ruskin. These included: Art is not a luxury; "Industry without art is brutality; life without industry is guilt" (these words of Ruskin's were later to become something of a mantra for Gill and Ananda Coomaraswamy); science ought to be wisdom and service; "There is no wealth but life"; economics should be a doctrine of wise production and beneficent distribution; education to be a tempering of the human spirit; the artist's proper office is to teach and inspire; nature is our garden home not a resource to exploit; property must observe propriety and quality of life as the end of all rational activity. These lessons gave Lethaby's views their moral and socialist bias.

Lethaby was one of many who responded to the seminal challenge of Ruskin's "The Nature of Gothic" that signaled the moral poverty of the division of labor. He was, both historically and intellectually, an intermediate figure who marked the transition from the pioneers of the Arts and Crafts movement, to the later generation, who turned their back on the "antiquarianism" of the pioneers in order to come to rational terms with the needs of a society based on industrial production. This was nothing more than to follow what Lethaby called the "scientific method".

It was an important observation of Lethaby's when he noted, in his essay "Design and Industry" (1915), that "it has been extremely unfortunate that the Arts and Crafts movement in England coincided in time with the violent fashion for antiques of every kind". This had led, he saw, to an obsession with design as a matter predominantly of style. This was simply "unreasonable", and indeed untenable in an age having to cope with the increasing mechanization of production.

He was surely right when he claimed that "style" was nothing more than "a museum name for a past phase of art"; and he was certainly reasonable in saying that "rightly understood, 'design' is not an agony of contortion but an effort to arrive at what will be obviously fit and true". From this argument he concluded "that there is as little reason for an architect [artist/craftsman, one might add] to pretend to work in a style than there is for a chemist". It might be said that the idea which presided over all Lethaby's endeavors was his hope to combine two realities, "the reality of natural necessity and common experience with the reality of the philosophers, which is the ideal, and to reconcile again Science with Art". It is what Lethaby understood by the "ideal" that kept him apart from modernism, even though he was later claimed by the modernists as one of their pioneers.

In the early years of his professional life Lethaby was in the habit of holidaying in Northern France, where, as Priscilla Johnston records in her memoir of him, "he studied and drew . . . with devotion and the insight for which he was noted, divining things that had escaped all other observers. He mentally put himself in the position, and almost inside the minds of the old masons. He knew why they did what they did except for the fraction which no one could know." This training, coupled with his exceptional insight, fed the central concern of his writings on art and labor. These are perhaps the most important parts of his legacy, and alone make him a significant figure in that long line of thinkers and practitioners, from William Blake to the present day, whose dissenting voice has challenged the intellectual, imaginative, and practical premises of industrial society.

Following Ruskin, Lethaby's central insight was to see that art and manual work are at the heart of life: "As work is the first necessity of existence, the very center of gravity of our moral system, so a proper recognition of work is a necessary basis of all right religion, art, and civilization. Society becomes diseased in direct ratio to its neglect and contempt of labor." He went so far as to propose, in his essay "The Foundation of Labor" (1917), a sort of National Service of manual work, with the intention that it should teach reverence for labor as the basis of art, "for art is the labor which is fully worthy of reverence". If all those who intended to live by "brain-work" were to give themselves to such a service, if this was the basis of their actual experience, then "perhaps we might hope to control the machines before they

tear civilization to bits". What lay behind this prescriptive challenge was Lethaby's belief that the arts had become too separated
from life and suffered from isolation and professionalism. Art had
become too specialized—"no great art is only one man deep".
Fine art had become free at the expense of what he called "work-
art", for in the making of necessary things there can be no freedom
from labor, utility, and service. Such a pretended freedom is in
reality an isolating of life from the body. Art is not limited to the
manifestation of aesthetic essence. As Lethaby claimed in "The
Foundation of Labor":

> Historically, the word Art has meant work, production, making,
> doing, and it was not conceived that the spirit, the expression,
> the meaning of the several kinds of work could be separated
> from a residuum which without it becomes brute labor. Art is
> the *substance* as well as the *expression*; it is the *service* as well
> as the *delight*; and the two aspects cannot be torn apart except
> to the ruin of both.

In "Art and Workmanship" (1913) he came nearest to a defin-
itive formulation of his ideas on the nature of art. Dismissing the
"sham technical twaddle" (Morris' words) of much art criticism,
he stood by his beliefs.

> There is nothing occult about the thought that all things may
> be made well or made ill. It may be a well-made statue or a
> well-made chair, or a well-made book. Art is not a special sauce
> applied to ordinary cooking; it is the cooking itself if it is good.
> Most simply and generally art may be thought of as the *well-
> doing of what needs doing*. If the thing is not worth doing it can
> hardly be a work of art, however well it may be done. A thing
> worth doing which is ill done is hardly a thing at all.

Needless to say, Lethaby saw that any revaluation of the nature
and place of art and workmanship in life must necessarily raise the
question of the nature and function of Beauty. In this he was no
different from Ruskin and Morris before him, or from Johnston,
Gill, and Coomaraswamy after him. Lethaby almost shies away
from any head-on discussion of beauty, partly because he was all
too aware of what might happen—*had* happened—whenever

artists, craftsmen, and architects make the pursuit of beauty their direct and overriding goal. As he wrote in "What Shall We Call Beautiful?" (1918): "As with the man who inquired whether he had yet attained wisdom, so with anxiety about enjoying beauty, the answer must ever be, 'It might have been, if you had not thought about it'. Beauty has to come by the way."

As we shall see, what underpins this last remark and all of Lethaby's observations and strictures on the subject of beauty is the ancient truth that beauty as such is not directly accessible to man apart from the truth of its presence in *things*. The workman's sole concern is with the good making of things, such that beauty cannot be isolated as a pursuable good in isolation from the authenticity of the process of its material embodiment.

It is better that men let beauty take care of itself—another axiom which Gill inherited from Lethaby—in the context of its being "the necessary function of fitness". It is the "smile of health" as he said elsewhere, rather than a shade of rouge. Just as he called for an understanding of art as the principle of perfect workman- ship *in* the artist, and not something applied to aesthetic feelings and enjoyment, so Lethaby called for a recognition of beauty as an idea arising incidentally out of the pursuit of those qualities that ought to be exercised in the making of true art: service, fitness of purpose, skill, economy, concentration, intensity, order, unity, as well as realization and identity with the values of past excellence. Just as there is danger in isolating art from utility, so is there in any activity intended to embody beauty when it is divorced from service, production, and creation. The following, from "What Shall We Call Beautiful?" has as much finality as any statement he pronounced on the subject: "Beauty in Art is the evidence of high humanity in work. Appreciation of Beauty should be one with our judgment of essential quality; there should be an instant recognition of what is noble and what is base. The sense of Beauty is the work-conscience." Thus for him it was merely to state the obvious to say "every work of art shows that it was made by a human being for a human being. Art is the humanity put into workmanship, the rest is slavery". This is more or less the starting point for Gill who, in calling beauty the "splendor of Being", shifts the emphasis away from the affective and towards the cognitive: "In things of beauty the mind comes into its own." Indeed, in the context of his Scholastic way of thinking Gill ends by identifying beauty with holiness; "Beauty is holiness made visible."

In what has been presented of Lethaby's ideas so far, we have hardly gone beyond anything that Morris advocated. Both thought that machines could relieve men from drudgery, but Lethaby was prepared to go further and to allow that the artist/craftsman might provide good models for machine production.[1]

Lethaby's ambivalence towards the role and value of machines in human society was forced upon him by a situation he confronted in his essay "Art and Workmanship": "We cannot go back" as "we cannot stay where we are". In "The Foundation of Labor" he aired something of his dilemma, that though the machine had "come to stay" none the less it was a "wrecking force in the world" that had "swiftly changed the character of our population". He was even prepared to predict that the world will "in fact, be shattered by it". He therefore called for its control, on the basis that "mass production" implies "production for the mass". In the face of *laissez-faire* production by the owners of machinery, society in turn has "as much right to control any form of machinery as we

---

[1] Johnston was no less sensitive to the dilemma of the situation, but was only partially in favor of the craftsman collaborating with mass production. To prepare punches "for printer's type or any similar form of work intended for limited reproduction . . . I am in favor of it, but *designing* things for others to make (such as my designing of some type faces) is apt to be a dangerous game", he wrote to Noel Rooke in 1933. He thought "*mass production as commonly understood . . . an evil, mitigated perhaps if it is in the nature of a transition method essential as a forerunner to a better state of civilization.*"

The degree of ambiguity in both Lethaby's and Johnston's (as well as others') views on the seemingly intractable problem of the proper relationship between the craftsman who creates one-off works on the one hand, yet on the other might be called upon to provide designs for subsequent mass production by machines, is indicative of a problem that possibly cannot be resolved in such detail as finally to remove any question of operating double standards. There are matters in life that will always escape precise formulation. Johnston's statement here is a case in point. He appears of be saying that, in designing a punch the craftsman has a *direct* intellectual and aesthetic responsibility over a matrix from which duplicate types must be struck. It is not possible to print from the punch itself. However, to design a punch which is subsequently, in some way, manufactured by machine as a duplicate punch *and nothing more* would be a matter of "*designing* things for others to make".

have to protect ourselves from firearms". "Machinery must be controlled."

There can be little doubt that Lethaby's "fear" of the machine (and Johnston's and Gill's for that matter) rests upon an unpalatable truth that Morris had acknowledged in "Useful Work Versus Useless Toil" (1885):

> It is waste of time to try to express in words due contempt of the production of the much-praised cheapness of our epoch. It must be enough to say that this cheapness is necessary to the system of exploiting on which modern manufacture rests. In other words, our society includes a great mass of slaves, who must be fed, clothed, housed, and amused as slaves, and that their daily necessity compels them to make the slave-wares whose use is the perpetuation of their slavery.

There can be no less doubt that Lethaby had arrived at *the* intractable problem of the modern world: is the machine to be the master or servant of man? The very nature of Lethaby's polemic against a world he saw was destroying the very basis of civilized community makes some assessment of that polemic inevitable.

Lethaby saw everything through the eye of an architect possessing an uncommon empathy with and insight into the many related crafts of the building trades. It was his concern that the study and practice of architecture should be freed from the pursuit of "style", which led him to the necessarily interconnected question of what constitutes the proper nature of art and workmanship. It meant asking, what art is *in principle* before it becomes an idea put into practice, before it is applied; even before it becomes, as he believed it to be, the most noble response to human requirements—that which satisfies man's spiritual needs.

To satisfy this latter function Lethaby saw that art must in some sense embody an intelligible symbolism. In his little book *Architecture*, first published in 1911, he spoke of this embodiment in buildings as inspiring "awe" and "wonder": not as an applied element, but as arising out of the fitness of the work. "In becoming fit", he said, "every work attains some form and enshrines some mystery". He also saw that this enshrined mystery ultimately depends upon a "heavenly prototype"—that is, the expression of an idea of archetypal reality. It most emphatically was not to enshrine some antiquarian style.

It must be said that Lethaby was always reticent about what he thought the supreme mysteries comprised, and how man might actively, spiritually, engage with them. He only ever tacitly acknowledged the divine as being the ultimate principle according to which all human making and doing must be measured, and never went so far as to say that the divine is the fundamental reality on which all human experience rests. His book *Architecture, Nature, and Magic*[2] was a pioneering attempt to co-ordinate the universal symbolism by which, throughout the ages, men have sought to link themselves to the presiding realities beyond the passing world. Yet he was, as René Guénon noted in a review, unable to bring out the true significance of his material. Even the word "Magic", changed from "Myth" in the first edition, seems an equivocation. We search in vain for any statement in the whole of Lethaby's writings that gives us any idea of the interconnectedness of man and God. In his essay "Towns to Live In" (1918), he spoke of the arts as constructing "a ladder of salvation", but we are given no substantial idea as to the nature of the reality to which such a ladder might lead. Reading him we remain uncertain as to the extent of Lethaby's understanding of the ramifications of seeing man as essentially a spiritual being. In the "ideal" that Lethaby so frequently looked to, God is curiously hidden from sight as a participating cause in the fulfillment of man's work, being veiled by such notional realities as "rational construction", "necessities of material", "systems of craftsmanship", even a "scheme of related measurements".

His equivocation in this respect obliged him to concentrate, for the most part, on the external aspects of how the arts might serve to fulfill man's spiritual needs. Historically, this is understandable. The whole point of the Arts and Crafts movement out of which he grew was that unlike, say, the constructors of the

---

[2] Lethaby described the first edition of this work—published in 1892 as *Architecture, Mysticism, and Magic*—as the most ignorant book ever published. He later revised it as a series of articles in *The Builder* in 1928. This revised version was finally published in book form in 1956.

great cathedrals, who built to the limit of the science of their day (a science which, it must be acknowledged, possessed a qualitative dimension), Ruskin and Morris anxiously sought to arrest the decline of the crafts in the face of a science conceived and applied purely quantitatively, which was already well on the way to eliminating the human altogether from any productive process. This same movement called, in Lethaby's generation, for a rearguard action wholly against the grain of the times. Lethaby saw that a stylistic antiquarianism—the "treadmill of style mongering", as he called it—was no answer. Accepting that the modern maker possesses no effective symbolic language with which to construct a "ladder of salvation", Lethaby proposed what amounts to a species of practical humanism. Such questions as fitness of form, reasonableness, service, practical necessity, economic viability (provided that the economics were not allowed wholly to determine the nature and purpose of supply and demand), and a qualified use of design for such subsequent machine manufacture as he espoused, move him in the direction of modern functionalism. From Lethaby's standpoint, however, modernism throws out the baby with the bath water in rejecting, more or less, any question of beauty other than of a utilitarian function. His rejection of the aesthetic notion of art, coupled with his qualified acceptance of the machine, places Lethaby awkwardly vis-à-vis modernism. With modernism, machine facture becomes the norm for nearly all production and it is the crafts that are relegated to the limbo of antiquarianism. Lethaby and modernism both lack a proper philosophy of man, with the difference that Lethaby needs such a philosophy before he can hope to establish a hierarchy of human needs based on something more substantial (salvational, one might say) than human appetites. Merely to cater for "wants" is not necessarily to satisfy needs. Utilitarian modernism, on the other hand, needs a philosophy of man if it is ever to do more than cater for market expediency. The alienating utility of our abundant mass-produced goods, which people have had no hand in making but are persuaded through advertising to consume, does nothing to satisfy man's spiritual needs. Saleability is no criterion for a standard of human fulfillment.

All this is a long way from finding the spiritual satisfaction in art and labor that was available to the men who built the cathedrals which Lethaby so admired and so carefully studied. Theirs was a culture in which it was still possible to relate human workmanship to a cosmic and redemptive paradigm, as Coomaraswamy, in the decades before and after Lethaby's death in 1931, demonstrated with a thoroughness of scholarly detail not available to Lethaby.

In defining art as everything that is rightly done or made, Lethaby certainly drew on the traditional doctrine whereby art is the principle of perfected work. But his lack of a proper doctrine of man left him in a position where he could never effectively show what agency or set of principles were appealed to in order to establish what is "right". It is man who knows what is right, and man who is guided by the values and meanings embodied in what is right. This cannot be done by a simple appeal to his creaturehood. That is to enthrone self-will. Having learned much from the older man, Gill went beyond Lethaby's position in recognizing that the human is, finally, only definable in terms of the Divine: "Strange fact! Man cannot live on the human plane; he must be either above it or below it", he wrote, following the Scholastic dictum, "*Homo non proprie humanus sed superhumanus est*". In the sphere of making and doing, paradoxically, man does not reach to the superhuman by the supposed virtues of self-willed achievement, but falls into the subhuman. Man is either created in the image of God, and that fact will determine the nature and extent of his needs; or he is a congeries of appetites, ever reluctant to accept a curb on their natural exertion.

From Lethaby's position this was an horizon too far. He saw that human needs must be satisfied in and through the art of noble workmanship. But his reticence towards "the Kingdom of God" (that which, as the Bible reminds us, must be sought first) meant that for his philosophy needs are, in effect, based on little more than the interweaving currents of social events and man's natural inclination to make things in the economic context of those events. This is the road to consumerism which, when straightened and broadened, gives us what we have now: a meaningless superfluity (at least in the "developed world") that in its unrestrained abundance threatens to engulf us—precisely the eliminating of the human at the heart of life that Lethaby saw and hoped to arrest.

Lethaby ends the chapter "The Temple of Heaven" in his *Architecture, Nature, and Magic* with a nostalgic passage that looks back to the monuments of earliest cultures, while coupling an appeal to the mere humanity of "sense" with a note of defeat at the prospect immediately before him. But the chapter's final question mark denotes an impotence which we continue to share:

> Our western architectural methods of designing whim-works in the sham styles can hardly compete with such symbolical art; common sense is the only way open to us. Those ancient works were imitations of paradise, ours are exercises in commercial "grandeur" and advertising vulgarity. Design must have some motivating *idea* in it: what idea can we modern people think except structure for reasonable service?[3]

In his essay on Lethaby, the critic Peter Fuller concluded that he failed to supply a "solution" to the problem "of how men and women's aesthetic and spiritual needs can be met in a modern, secular, technological society". We must immediately note that this accusation harbors two unwarranted assumptions: that such needs *can* be met in a modern, secular, technological society, and, if a "solution" were to be offered, that it would inevitably be adopted and adapted to perform its remedial function. History knows otherwise when it comes to such assumptions.

Moreover, and more importantly, this accusation seems to demand, impossibly, that an effect be delivered of its cause. The modern, secular, technological society *is* precisely the outcome of man's aesthetic and spiritual needs being suppressed and ignored.

---

[3] A decade or so after Lethaby's death the work of several scholars began to demonstrate the direct interaction of the Divine in man's attempt to build according to a heavenly paradigm. See for instance Erwin Panofsky, *Abbot Suger on the Abbey Church of St. Denis and its Treasures* (Princeton: Princeton University Press, 1946), Otto von Simson, *The Gothic Cathedral* (New York: Pantheon, 1962), Titus Burckhardt, *Chartres and the Birth of the Cathedral* (original German edition 1962, English translation, Bloomington, IN: World Wisdom Books/Ipswich: Golgonooza, 1995), Louis Charpentier, *The Mysteries of Chartres Cathedral* (New York: Avon Books, 1975), as well as, later, Rene Querido, *The Golden Age of Chartres* (Edinburgh: Floris, 1987), and the studies in sacred geometry of Keith Critchlow, John James, Robert Lawlor, and others.

There can be no "solution" on the level of application that is the legitimate sphere of making and doing. *What* is to be "solved" is beyond the jurisdiction of the maker as such. The maker's wisdom is a type of knowledge about skill applied to some productive end. The wisdom about what can be a solution to satisfying man's spiritual needs belongs to a type of knowledge that includes a vision of the final end of human life. Such a vision is not in the sphere of making and doing. Action comes into its own on the basis of a prior knowledge. Speaking from the standpoint of the maker, Morris warned in "Useful Work Versus Useless Toil":

> To attempt to answer such questions thoroughly or authoritatively would be attempting the impossibility of constructing a scheme of a new society out of the materials of the old, before we knew which of those materials would disappear and which endure through the evolution which is leading us to the great change.

Lethaby's position was no different from that of Ruskin and Morris before him, and Gill, Coomaraswamy, Massingham, and many others after him. His vision of noble workmanship was defeated by the economics of the machine. The momentum of capitalist investment, in the pursuit of wealth, must ever seek to reduce the cost of production in the pursuit of a cash surplus. Thus by degrees the handiwork of the skilled worker is undermined by the use of machines. Such is the remorseless pressure of this process that it becomes, in due course, a sort of cannibalism, first of all destroying the machine minder through automation, then, in a further step, destroying the machine by an economy based on the virtual reality of computerized information. At this stage the question of human needs hardly arises, having been displaced by the internal demands of the productive system itself. This "system", possessing no vision of an end other than its own perpetuation, must eventually bring about its own destruction. Can we claim we have seen no intimation of this?

An economics of noble workmanship, such as Lethaby envisaged, allows quantity to yield to quality as part of a culture that acknowledges that the end of the productive process is above and beyond the process itself. The most precious commodity of the craftsman is time free from economic constraint. Capitalist economics demands that quality yield to quantity. Time must yield to a surplus of money. What takes time in the exercise of skill must be converted to a technique that produces more and faster. This technique will begin by approximating to human skill and end by replacing skill altogether in order to produce goods that no human skill could produce. There could never be such a thing as a "handcrafted" mobile telephone. What began as a way of duplicating human skill on a greater scale ends as a means to produce goods regardless of any human intervention. By now the "market" demands that it should be so. Gill used to say that machines are not designed to produce things but the thing called profit!

As a necessary part of this process any call for the control of machines, however desirable in human terms, is bound to seem illogical since it amounts to the destruction of the system for generating the wealth needed to perpetuate the consumption that underpins the social fabric. When Lethaby, in "The Arts and the Function of the Guilds" (1896), called for the Trades Unions to become supervisors of the quality of commodities, he assumed that "Society generally", as he put it, would "soon pay back the debt in sympathy". It is just conceivable that this might have been possible at the end of the nineteenth century. It is a vain hope in our time. Lethaby's call for quality rests on the assumption that the consumer is sufficiently cultivated to recognize and use skill after its own kind. But there is no such thing as an understanding by "society generally". Each and every man and woman understands according to individual ability. The consumer of manufactured goods is himself a patron of skill to the extent his purchasing power, and the way in which he exercises it, determines what and how things get made—and at what price. If, as patron, he has long since been dispossessed of any intellectually responsible involvement in the making and using of the commodities of life, then he will have no standard by which to recognize the qualitative from the shoddy. In such a situation he is unlikely to envisage any imperative of debt towards his fellows—consumers and producers—in a situation where the commodities available to him show little or no sign of having been made with an eye to stimulating any sense of the nobility of his human calling.

This is the self-crippling position we are in today, inundated as we are with the consequences of having perfected, beyond the dreams of previous generations, techniques for producing over-abundant, meaningless superfluities. Ruskin's claim that "industry without art is brutality" needs revision. In a society where labor hardly any longer exists (having been exported to Third World countries) industry without art has become a mind-numbing palliative of time-serving hardly made bearable by the constant distractions of the "leisure industry", all in the name of an economic growth devoid of moral direction, whose social injustice and material unsustainability is self-evident. There are no "solutions" without responsibilities and those must take root in the conscience of each and every one of us.

Which brings us to the question of greed.

3

Archetype as Letterform:

The "Dream" of Edward Johnston

During the many hours which I have spent in conversation with calligraphers and lettercutters over the years, I have always been struck by the way in which the practicalities of achieving the "perfect" letterform and its appropriate spacing in a given context are at the root of their preoccupation and effort. No doubt this is as it should be. What scribe or lettercutter worth his or her salt would take up this exacting craft and not be haunted and challenged by the idea of perfection?

But what one rarely comes across, if at all, is a serious consideration of *where* the notion of perfection comes from. For it has also been my experience that calligraphers and lettercutters, whilst pursuing their craft as if some notion of perfection was at least tacitly motivating them, are all too ready to deny that the perfect letterform exists.

What I would like to attempt here, then, is an exploration of the idea that the perfect letterform must be real—for if it were not, then it would not have the power to inspire the hand, the eye, and the mind of the craftsman as often as it obviously does.[1] Perhaps it would be better to say that the perfect letterform has a reality, even if it is never manifest in a material substance, such as ink or stone, or to use more Scholastic terms, that it has *being* even if it does not *exist*. But to make this distinction between being and existence presupposes that reality is much more complex and multi-layered than what our everyday consciousness reveals to us.

---

[1] The reference throughout to a perfect letterform is more a matter of convenience than a dogmatic assertion. This same perfection is operative in a whole collection of letters that, cumulatively, have an organic unity, each single letter being in some way modified in accommodation to the whole context of its presence.

You may be familiar with the old adage that "to work is to pray", a saying which gives some indication of the fact that the crafts were traditionally practiced as if it were possible that they possessed a spiritual dimension and that they might act as a support for contemplation. I believe the writings of Edward Johnston indicate that he exercised his vocation as if this was still a possibility. Even though Johnston's practical example has inspired innumerable scribes to take up calligraphy and lettering, no one, so far as I know, has so far examined this aspect of his work. If it is time to re-examine the legacy of Johnston (as has been suggested by some contemporary lettering practitioners), then this rather more "hidden" aspect ought to be fundamental to that re-examination.

If calligraphy is to be understood and practiced as being more than a game of shape-forming—albeit a very skilful and sophisticated game—then we might look to the example of Johnston to learn more of the depths of this ancient, universal craft. Johnston's was an example that prompted one of his pupils to claim of his inspirational teaching that it came as if out of "eternity and infinity" (L147).[2] That is a very pointed description, whose wording is carefully chosen. Speaking of the ultimate objective of his work, Johnston himself said: "Life is the thing we all want and it is the desire for life that is behind all religion and all art. . . . Our aim should be . . . to make letters live . . . that men themselves may have more life" (P88). Again, we note the carefully chosen words. This does not sound like someone advocating the practice of "art for art's sake", or even "craft for craft's sake".

If you look at your copy of *Writing and Illuminating, and Lettering*—that is, if you have an earlier edition—you will find three quotations given prominence on a page facing the Author's

---

[2] The abbreviations used throughout are an initial followed by the page number of the following books by Johnston: F = *Formal Penmanship and Other Papers*, edited by Heather Child (London: Lund, Humphries, 1971); L = *Lessons in Formal Writing*, edited by Heather Child and Justin Howes (New York: Taplinger Publishing Company, 1986); P = Priscilla Johnston, *Edward Johnston* (second edition, New York: Taplinger Publishing Company, 1976); W = *Writing and Illuminating, and Lettering* (New York: The Macmillan Company, 1906), and reprinted many times.

Preface. (I have a copy of the 23rd edition of this book in which this page was still included. At some later date it was withdrawn.)

Now from all that we know of him we can certainly agree with Eric Gill's assessment that Johnston was "deliberate of speech and equally deliberate of thought". We know that Johnston was a deeply religious man, and it is therefore impossible to believe that he lived his life keeping his vocation as a calligrapher and his religious experience in separate compartments. So we must believe that these quotations were chosen with great deliberation by a man who claimed that the "one thing I care most about" is "to search out and live the truth" (P34). We must also remember that Johnston thought sufficiently of the following passage to write it out at least twice in 1934, one of these being for presentation to no less a master craftsman than Alfred Fairbank. Of this Johnston said, "in many ways the ms is yet my best" (L35). The last of the three quotations reads as follows: "In that communion only, beholding beauty with the eye of the mind, he will be enabled to bring forth, not images of beauty but realities (for he has hold not of an image but of a reality), and bringing forth and nourishing true virtue to become a friend of God and be immortal, if mortal man may" (Wx).

This extraordinary passage, taken from Plato's *Symposium* and given such prominence by Johnston, needs to be examined carefully. I say "extraordinary" because it is by no means representative of the habits of mind and thought that have shaped and which energize the modern world, referring as it does to the intelligible realm of archetypal Ideas. Indeed, it is precisely because Johnston placed at the head of his treatise a quotation which does not underwrite modern assumptions as to the nature of reality and the mind[3] that we must look at that quotation in some detail.

---

[3] For instance, we find the following "Argument" in Johnston's *A Carol and Other Rhymes* (London: Hampshire House Workshops, 1915), pp. 48-50, which gives some indication of the nature of his thought in this matter:

> We see the light of the stars, not the stars themselves: we see the light reflected from a piece of white paper, not the paper itself. In other words, we see what things are *doing* rather than what they *are*. But as light takes time to travel—however short the distance—it is more exact to say that

The passage occurs in that part of Plato's dialogue where Diotima is elaborating for Socrates her teaching that Love is "a great spirit between divine and mortal". She says that it is possible for men to gaze on Beauty's very self, unsullied, "not dogged with the pollution of mortality and all the colors and varieties of human life". Diotima insists that, only when men discern heavenly beauty itself—face to face—through what makes it visible, will they have hold of the true.

The quotation begins, "In that communion"—that is to say, in the mind's *contemplation* of beauty, and continues, "beholding beauty with the eye of the mind". When he speaks of "mind" here Plato does not, as might be assumed, mean the rational mind—that part of our common-sense consciousness that makes a reasoned judgment about things on the basis of empirical observation and logical calculation. And the "eye" referred to is not the eye of sensible apprehension—for Plato, like Heraclitus before him, held that the senses are unreliable witnesses when it comes to discerning what is unchangingly true. The "eye of the mind" is an intuitive faculty of the soul, which permits it to grasp metaphysical and spiritual realities which are not subject to change, as is every reality conditioned in whatever way by time and space. "To bring forth" means to grasp and hold with unwavering stability a truth of the mind beyond the world of the senses. It is, as

we see what things *have been doing*. This is the way in which we "see" all material objects, whether "near" or "far", but it is impressed on us in the case of the stars, because we understand that the light of the nearest star—our Sun—takes over eight minutes to reach the Earth, and the light from the Sun's nearest neighbor nearly four years, while the flight of the light from the great majority of stars, it is said, "is to be reckoned in hundreds of years". Truly, though we see the star shine, we can hardly say that we see the stars shining (the action of our bodily sight, therefore, is an act of faith—for Faith is "the evidence of things not seen").

If we see, then, in the material world only what a thing is doing—or has done—but not the thing itself, how may we hope that our Love, or Faith, or Hope will ever discover its objective? Divine Love—which knows all Things—IS, and therefore does not depend on time to reach things, or on that which we call "nearness"—and in the very word confess distance.

In the heart of Man there is the shining of all his "stars"—those "stars" which he cannot reach, or even see with his bodily eyes—but yet he may be in touch with them—Divine Love in his heart sees the stars for him.

Plato goes on to say, to grasp "a reality" as opposed to "an image" (or representation) of beauty. Plato is pointing out that external appearances, because they are the very fabric of which transient reality is woven, have something illusory or deceptive about them. He is making the distinction between that which possesses true, permanent Being, and things which exists only in the mind as a mental abstraction. So, when he speaks of "bringing forth and nourishing" he is referring to the archetypal truths that enter into one's very being so as to become part of our very identity, rather than truths of a more ephemeral nature that are temporarily registered in the imagination as a transient image. When the contemplator is truly absorbed into these archetypal truths or Ideas, he or she becomes, as Diotima continues, "the friend of God and . . . immortal". That is to say, the contemplator assumes or takes on the identity of the archetypal or of the Divine within, to the extent he or she is able to shed the grosser demands and predilections of the empirical ego.

An early familiarity with the idea that an approach to the Divine entails the sacrifice of one's ego is reflected in the fact that at the age of twenty-five, in 1897, Johnston wrote on a parchment, "The best way to see Divine Light is to put out your own candle" (L79).

Now all this may seem a far cry from the practice of calligraphy, but that it was important to Johnston we cannot doubt. What we must hold clearly in our minds is the truth that this contemplation of, and entering into, objective beauty is the grasping of a reality that is never materially embodied. It is an intuitive, unanalyzable experience that is known directly without the intervention of mediate, mental activity—that is, without any sort of mental calculation that effectively puts a distance between, or distinguishes, the knower and the known. It may be difficult for the modern mind, with its rational and materialist training and bias, to see that such archetypal Ideas are more true and more real than the products of mental calculation on the one hand, or physical realities on the other. But Johnston's belief that this is so becomes evident from a careful reading of the relevant passages of his writings. That he was more a Platonist[4] than a modernist also goes a long way to explain why he was increasingly at odds with the progressive, industrial world that surrounded him.

To help us get an idea of how this archetypal reality might apply to letterforms, we can turn to a passage in Johnston's *Writing and Illuminating, and Lettering.* He says: "The mere taking to pieces, or analyzing, followed by 'putting together', is only a means of becoming acquainted with the mechanism of con-struction, and will not reproduce the original beauty of a thing" (Wxix). In other words, that part of the mind that calculates, measures, and co-ordinates what the interaction of the hand, the eye, and the mind must apply in the making of a letterform does not go deep enough in itself to touch upon the "original beauty" of the perfect letterform that is none the less sought, whether implicitly or explicitly, in the craftsman's pursuit of the "perfect" letterform. This impalpable, archetypal letter (as we might call it), which lives in the deep recesses of the "eye of the mind", is what actually underpins the perfect unity of that physical and mental action required to shape palpably beautiful letters in whatever substance. When a manifestly beautiful letter is fully realized by the craftsman, then the archetype is, as it were, sounded so that what results is a letterform whose beauty reduces the observer to silence, unable to describe or quantify that in which its perfection consists. And, conversely, I would suggest that whenever we look at a letter that appears insufficient in some way, even though all its elements are "correctly" present, then in that experience of impoverishment we are intuitively sensing the absence of any reverberation of the archetypal "original beauty" which Johnston refers to.

Here, in parenthesis, it is interesting to note that in a Report on Art Schools that W. R. Lethaby prepared in 1898, a few months before meeting Johnston, he wrote: "Lettering of all kinds is almost without exception *bad*. Such students as endeavor to apply lettering harmoniously to their designs seem to endeavor to

---

[4] It might be noted that Robert Speaight, in his biography of Eric Gill, records Johnston reading Plato aloud to Gill in his workshop when they were close neighbors in Hammersmith.

invent new and contorted forms out of their heads. Of all things the form of letters has been shaped by tradition and in most cases the effort to be original is an effort to be *bad*" (P12).

Lethaby is surely noting here that such *bad* letterforms arise from the use only of that superficial part of the rational mind (if that!) that takes to pieces, analyzes, and puts together the basic elements of letters on the basis of personal preference. And when he says that the forms of letters have been shaped by tradition—with the implication that such forms are "good" and "beautiful"—it would surely be bad logic to interpret Lethaby as meaning that such forms are arrived at simply on the basis of habits of past precedent. An ugly or bad letterform does not acquire beauty or legitimacy in the process of being copied and repeated, for however long. Beauty is of another order than the mere passage of time.

Johnston himself, early in his career, defined "Beauty" as "obedience made manifest to the Laws of Truth" (P134)—we note the use of capitals on the words Beauty, Laws, and Truth. He did not significantly change his mind in later life, even though he went on to investigate those laws exactingly, testing them again and again against rigorous thought and assiduous practice. He never lost sight either of the earthly/heavenly axis along which, traditionally, the practice of any craft proceeds. Speaking of the old scribes at their work, he remarked that even more than their skill and the *speed* with which they wrote—as if writing an ordinary letter—and even though they were "engaged on serious work" and were not concerned with "art" as we think of it, "they had in their hearts a kind of dream of divine beauty that they were seeking . . . [and] . . . note how much that dream was fulfilled" (P153). Let us look a little closer at this "dream".

All that we know of Johnston presents us with a picture of an entirely practical man. There was nothing "abstract" or "airy-fairy" about him, nothing "arty". Indeed, we might doubt whether there was anything about him that was superficial. "Preoccupied", certainly, as the notice he made for his study door proclaimed, aimed at repelling unwelcome visitors. His daughter Priscilla said of him that "for all his lassitude he was extremely forceful, indeed dominant. It was not an active forcefulness of vitality but a kind of latent forcefulness of character" (P125).

But his was no utilitarian practicality. Johnston's vision of his craft begins at the beginning. By this I mean literally the beginning of all things—his testing of his ideas took him that far. Noel Rooke reports of him that "he related his subject to everything in heaven and earth" because he saw it as essentially part of a whole. Even when it came to describing a single element of letter formation—that of contrast—he took the comprehensive view: "Contrast is at the very root of formal penmanship. So is harmony. That is why our work, when well done, is so sparkling. It has that unique possession, the best of both sides; the idea of Heaven and Earth is there, harmony and contrast" (L176).

And Priscilla Johnston relates that her father once spoke to her of his taking a class, "of how he was able to give (the students) the feeling that it really was worth doing and a little of his vision, also, the spirit of it, over and above the technical side. He quoted *Man shall not live by bread alone* and spoke of the excitement of the vision" (P263). Can we not sense in this passage Johnston's desire to communicate the idea that the perfection of work which is the aim of the true craftsman must involve more that the mastery of practical skills, if indeed the craftsman is to become "a friend of God" as the quotation from Plato puts it?

Since man is created in the Divine Image (as Johnston believed), it follows that in the exercise of his vocation, the craftsman, by analogy, shares in the actions of the making of the world by its Creator. Johnston thought of the process of creation as involving three stages: "embodying , animating, and inspiring". The three stages must be understood and actualized in the context of man's origin and place in the fabric of the Creation. "In a book for craftsmen", Johnston wrote, "the primary order is Genesis 2:7: 'And the Lord God formed man of the dust of the ground, and breathed into his nostrils the breath of life; and man became a living soul'" (L47). Also in connection with man's being created in the Divine Image, Johnston asks us to consider Genesis 2:19, where it is related how God formed every beast and bird and how Adam named every living creature. That is to say, the word by which each thing is named establishes the unique and permanent reality of that thing. In the naming, by Adam, of each thing inheres the archetypal essence or Idea of that thing as it exists in the mind of God: as it exists in the Word, that is, the *logos*—the eternal reason of things. The scribe, giving a manifest form to true and beautiful words, recapitulates the Adamic action of giving each thing God's signature. Thus, named things and meanings co-inhere. And in this co-inherence is the very ligature that binds man to Truth itself. Johnston, true to his life-long insistence that the scribe pay attention to the meanings of the words he writes, is reported as having worn out his dictionary.

How Johnston saw Adam's giving of God's signature to each thing as an analogy of the scribe's action is clearly seen in the following passage: "All his [the craftsman's] works express Idea [note the Platonic capital, denoting a pre-existing, immaterial potentiality] . . . by substance brought to [material] life—like Adam made of Earth. Each of his [man's] works—like every son of Adam—bears a human touch and is seen to be unique. All things are unique, but the craftsman's works show this—each one [each manuscript of ours] is an autograph" (F141).

As each man bears the signature of God in his deiformity, so each work from the hand of the scribe bears the signature of its creator. Thus it is, infallibly and authentically, a thing brought materially to life from a pre-existing idea in the mind. This analogical wisdom is surely what resonates in Johnston's assertion that the proper task of the scribe is "to make letters live . . . that men themselves may have more life" (P88).

In a letter quoted by Priscilla Johnston, Johnston himself spoke of the *final creative act* as one in which God saw that the Creation was Good—"in fact, a thing is not completely created until it has been appreciated . . . I believe it" (P256). Here Johnston is at his most profound, for he is drawing upon the idea that the final justification for the Creation of the world, by God, is in the realization of the necessity that it is completed by being *known*. It is the responsibility of the craftsman's share in the Divine Creation to see that his work is good, that it is true, for it is the Truth, "both immanent and transcendent" (P308) that prevails. And of Truth, Johnston wrote: "its other names are goodness and beauty, the way and the Life, the Light (of the world), the Word, and many more." Which brings us to the question of beauty.

We can only understand Johnston's view of beauty correctly if we keep it in the context in which he himself placed it: Beauty is approached and found indirectly in the search for Truth, through the discipline of a proper utility of human needs. Priscilla Johnston reports her father as holding that "Beauty is an ultimate Grace which will be conferred upon the craftsman's work if it be well done. If Truth . . . has been served, the result will be Beauty" (L48). Can anyone look at the best of Johnston's works and not see that it is beautiful?

However that may be, it perhaps takes a more trained eye to see that the beauty of his forms arises out of their construction. It remained axiomatic for Johnston that "unless the design arises out of the actual construction of a thing it is reduced to the level of extraneous ornamentation. Design is inherent rather than applied . . ." (P285).

In connection with this principle we might incidentally note that Johnston's reluctance to have his work reproduced was precisely because of the resulting inauthenticity. As he pointed out, "nothing is reproduced, something different is produced" (P285).

As with design, so with the "original Beauty" of a thing. It is not something applied to the surface but comes out of workmanship honestly and straightforwardly undertaken. What, then, does such workmanship entail?

Like Gill, Johnston anchors his answer to all questions that have to do with the validity of the craftsman's activity by going back to the nature of the agent doing the work. What is man? Man is a creature, a body—"the flesh is a *sine qua non* for the spirit of man" (P308)—who looks to God for the answers to the primary questions: What, How, and Why. Why should one, why ought one, why must one, make a thing? And by a "thing" Johnston meant both "*what we make* and *what we do*" (F141). Moreover "things are His [God's] will" (P308). By virtue of asking these questions, man is searching for Truth as well as tacitly proposing that an answer can be found. Other names for Truth are Goodness and Beauty. And Truth "is that against which we sin" (P308). (This thought—that the workman can sin in his actions—may go some way to account for Johnston's lassitude.)

In making a thing, the scribe "works in substances . . . with special tools and special methods. He also thinks in substances and in things, and in methods. . . , which direct the tools and form the thing out of the substance". The "prime purpose of writing is to be read". "His direct objective is to write well", so that the work produced is useful. In his primary duty to the author "the words are of the first importance", and with this in mind the scribe aims at a presentation that is beautiful. Such beauty for formal penmanship is achieved by "Sharpness, Unity, and Freedom". In this, his *direct* purpose, "the scribe keeps the idea of usefulness constantly before him". "Usefulness in this context, consists in legibility, fitness for purpose, and perfect presentation. The scribe follows after usefulness since, in the final analysis, the ultimate objective of usefulness is beauty" (F141-42).

So, given that the scribe has mastered all the necessary practical skills, this alone will not suffice to achieve the "original beauty" that must be sought by indirect means. "Original beauty" comes intuitively through concentration upon, and contemplation of, the archetypal Ideas that letterforms embody. The fact that Johnston wrote little on the subject of beauty is itself an indication of the fact that, by its very nature, it is a subject all but unteachable in any direct sense. The pursuit of beauty in isolation from its necessary alignment with truth and legitimate human needs has always been recognized by the wisest minds as being liable to lead men astray, into folly and self-indulgence. Nevertheless, something of what is involved in achieving the original beauty of living letters can be glimpsed in words which Johnston addressed to an audience in Dresden in 1912. The passage occurs in a context touched upon earlier, regarding the scribe's aim to "make letters *live*". The relevant words are: "I think I can claim that, poor as they are, the letters on the blackboard are alive: that is not due to myself—I am only a superior kind of motor or engine—it is due to the pen [chalk!] (which brings life to letters)" (P187). It is "not due to myself": this attributing of his achievement in giving life to letters to a higher agency gives a hint, surely, of what is meant in the passage from Plato's *Symposium* by "nourishing true virtue to become a friend of God"?

To come back to Johnston's "dream" and to end with a question. Priscilla Johnston, in her memoir of her father, quotes him as saying: "I see no successor who will put his life and heart into the work I love. There are plenty of *good* scribes to whom it is an occupation and a profession but apparently not *a preoccupation and a dream*" (P251, our emphasis). His daughter was inclined to dismiss this remark, but given its pointed wording can we be so sure? Does not another interpretation offer itself? To anyone with a deep religious conviction, such as Johnston possessed, the scribe's vocation must be more than an entertaining and diversionary activity. The whole man must be engaged. Could it be that Johnston found no one willing to attempt, through the craft of the pen, that degree of contemplation, beyond the empirical ego, that engages those "realities"—and not their semblances—that enable the craftsman to "bring forth and nourish true virtue"—that interpenetration of being and knowing that is a gazing upon the heavenly beauty face to face, in so far as "mortal man may"?

4

Eric Gill:

Towards a Holy Tradition of Work

When Eric Gill died at the age of fifty-eight in 1940 he left behind
a dozen or so books and many shorter polemical writings, over a
thousand wood-engravings, nine typeface designs, a considerable
amount of sculpture, stone and wood carvings, inscriptions, some
of the finest nude studies of the last century, as well as designs
for postage stamps, coins, books, at least one clock, a church,
and much else besides. No wonder that those who have written
about him since cannot agree in their judgment as to the most
enduring part of this legacy. About this perhaps Gill had his own
ideas. David Jones reports that Gill had once said to him: "What
I achieve as a sculptor is of no consequence—I can only be a
beginning—it will take generations, but if only the beginnings of
a reasonable, decent, holy tradition of work might be effected—
that is the thing." Moreover, his friend and mentor Ananda K.
Coomaraswamy wrote, "he invented a human way of working,
and found that it was that of all human societies. . . . This amounts
to saying that Eric's was not a personal point of view, but simply a
true one, that he had made his own. He was not 'thinking for himself' but assenting to credible propositions; and he was, accord-
ingly, a man of faith." There is a precedent then for pointing to
Gill's doctrine of the norm of workmanship as the most singular
part of his achievement. There is a consistent and coherent doctrine scattered among his writings. It needs extraction.[1]

Gill was all of a piece. You must take him whole or not at
all. You can no more detach his doctrine of art from his doctrine

---

[1] For this see *A Holy Tradition of Working: Passages from the Writings of Eric
Gill,* edited by Brian Keeble (Ipswich: Golgonooza Press, 1983). The present
essay is a slightly revised version of the accompanying introductory essay for this
anthology.

of work than you can detach his morals from his religion. They all go together. He cannot be tried against the prevailing conditions or the "inevitability of history" or against the acceptance of human culpability without those things thereby being seen the more clearly for what they are. His appeal is always to necessity and good sense.

Almost invariably, his past detractors have failed to perceive the level at which his thought moves. This failure on the part of many of his critics springs not so much from a mere disagreement about the purpose and direction of our civilization as from their unwillingness to accept the degree to which Gill's views are at one and the same time "absolute" and "radical".

Gill refused to put together a philosophy by way of accommodations and small adjustments to any of the modes and disguises with which the doctrine of a godless scientific and economic progress infiltrates the mental and physical life of modern society. Perhaps the more common form of capitulation to this "progress" is the passive acceptance with which it is believed that "machines are here to stay!" That Gill saw no such necessity, and that he saw their eventual demise as being due to their fundamental incompatibility with the proper nature of man has caused some of his critics to accuse him of wanting to go back to the Middle Ages. This criticism persists in spite of the fact that he has specifically written that there can be no putting back of the clock and that we must make the best of modern conditions on the basis of sheer reasonableness. Where the critic wants the convenience of what is familiar, and the compensations of "art", Gill simply wants truth and consistency. Gill had his sights on the heavenly Jerusalem: his critics have theirs on England today, or perhaps tomorrow. It is the perpetual clash of interests between the politics of eternity and the politics of time.

This clash of interests, having engaged Gill's critics in the past, must certainly engage his reader today. There have been two permanent stumbling-blocks between Gill and his reader. The two interlock. The first is the obvious need to come to terms with the absoluteness of his image of man: his quite literal belief in the fact that man is created in the image of God. If you believe this to be true, and you examine the consequences that follow from it as rigorously as Gill did, your conclusions as to the nature and purpose of human life must be totally different from those you would hold if you believe that man is a mere "higher", more clever primate, a more or less haphazard system of appetites, instincts, and energy drives and the like. This latter view is so obviously incompatible with the whole spectrum of Gill's thought that the reader must either learn to accommodate Gill on this point or admit that he desires other things and pass on.

The second stumbling-block—the assumption that the "progress" of technological development is inevitable—has already been touched upon. But the following must be added. If you assume that the whole of man's experience does not go beyond the world of time and space then you must believe that all development will take place within the confines of that world. In which case there can only be an exploration of the extent of space and—since the horizontal movement of time is ever forward—development in future time. The pull of the future must seem inevitable in such circumstances. It is hardly coincidental, therefore, that the philosophy of materialism (which rests upon such assumptions) should, as Gill says, "click" with an industrial world, and that in the nature of things it must issue in an ever greater degree of technological development and sophistication. But this did not prevent Gill from seeing the inconsistency of such a belief with free-will (with its concomitant of intellectual responsibility), and with the ultimately spiritual nature of man.

The two presiding principles with which Gill guides his thoughts on the nature and purpose of human making are those of "beauty" and "art". Let us look at his notion of beauty first. Here Gill's point of departure is St. Thomas, quoting St. Dionysius the Areopagite: "The Beauty of God is the cause of the being of all that is." Thus beauty is an absolute and has to do with cognition. Absolute Beauty is the very cause of the perfection of things and as being is coincident with the Good, is the end to which the nature of things tends. The Scholastic doctrine of beauty as a transcendental, an objective property in things—the splendor of intelligibility—can be traced back through St. Dionysius and Augustine to Plotinus and eventually to Plato's formulation of beauty as the radiance of truth. It was this tradition that St. Thomas built upon, but giving beauty a more immediate and subjective emphasis when he described it as "that which pleases when seen". But we must not assume that St. Thomas' deceptively simple description identifies beauty with that pleasure, that quickening of the aesthetic senses that is felt in common delight. Gill reminds us that what *sees* is the mind, the "inner eye" of the mind. Though the outward senses are the channel through which what pleases must pass, nevertheless in seeing beauty the mind acts and apprehends in the selfsame act Being Itself. In that act the *thing* that presents itself is not diffused or dissolved away into abstraction. It remains in the perfection and order proper to itself, a thing of greater clarity, a thing without which no beauty is seen at all. And this perfection and clarity is nothing less than the thing's essence, its form, the qualitative imprint, as it were, stamped on the created thing by its creator. Thus in the measure that a thing seen reflects the beauty proper to itself, so the mind sees what that thing is without adulteration and privation.

By analogy the same is true of works of art as things made, since whatever is made is first conceived in the mind of the artist. It is the intelligibility of this formative process in which the work of art is made in imitation of its mental prototype that the beauty of art consists. Just as the beauty of natural things is in accordance with the perfection of their being as part of the whole of the created order of things, so the beauty of a work of art is inseparable from its occasion and purpose as a thing called forth by intelligible need. Beauty cannot be said to be a property belonging to works of art exclusively, and the artist or workman does not proceed directly to "make beauty" any more than he works to "produce pleasure". The beauty of works of art is not aesthetic (as is our pleasure at the resultant thing), but cognitive and in accordance with the goodness and truth with which the said work fulfils what it is its nature to be. For this reason a work of art (or nature) is inseparable from its creator's intention, always remembering that as it is not part of God's intention to create natural things for the sake of idle curiosity, but to lead us on to higher things, so it should never be the intention of the artist to create meaningless luxuries which it is beneath man's natural dignity to tolerate.

The complementary principle to beauty in Gill's thought is that of art. Traditionally and normally, the notion of art is part of a body of wisdom according to which things made attain to the proper perfection of their nature. Man, considered in the light of an inverse metaphysical analogy whereby he is the reflected image of God, in fashioning an object materially at the same time fashions himself spiritually. By the same process of analogy, in the act of creating God externalizes Himself whereas the artist or workman in the act of making internalizes himself. By making outwardly, in an act of pure worship, man fashions his own internal essence. That is to say, he returns to the perfection of his own nature. Here we have the perennial idea of human vocation as part of the conformity of all things to their true nature as an expression of the Divine will. Only he can attain perfection who is integrated with the causes and ends of things. This way he incurs no sin—sin being defined as a departure from the order to the end. We might recall that in his *Republic*, Plato described justice as the freedom of men to do and act according to what it is their nature to be. And in connection with works *of* art Gill wrote: "We've got to make things right. Beauty consists in due proportion. We have got to give things the proportion that is due to them. It's a matter of justice." The artist works, then, in imitation of the true nature of things. He does not imitate God's works, for that would be to make copies of copies, but imitates God's manner of working as it is inherent in his nature so to do.

The word "art", in the scholastic formulation of the traditional wisdom, refers to that operative habit of the intellect by which the artist possesses what is the proper perfection of work to be done. This formulation takes as its point of departure Aristotle's description—in his *Nicomachean Ethics*—of art as the innate condition of the mind by which a man proceeds upon a rational course of action in the making of something. Art is the inner habit of skill, not mere outward dexterity. By the light of art the workman sees what is to be done; by the operation of art he knows how it shall be done. As the operative agent of art the workman's only concern is for the good of the work to be done. In departing from the perfecting of his art the workman sins as an artist. Art, then, stays in the artist and is not personified by the artist. David Jones observed of Gill that he worked as though a tradition existed. He meant that Gill worked assuming that these conditions and values both applied and were true.

With the division of "art" from "work" and "beauty" from "use" in the modern world, art comes out of the artist and gets attached, so to say, to the work of art itself. The creator of "art", now called an "artist", personifies art and is given the sole prerogative of its production. Beauty too comes out of the thing made to be an aesthetic sensation desired for its own sake. No longer the property of a thing that shows forth the fullness of integrity, harmony, and intelligible clarity due to its being; no longer identified with goodness and truth, beauty is now associated with a select category of things made. As an aid to emotional stimulus, beauty is freed from the process of rational manufacture so that art has become "pure" or "fine" and as such is treated idealistically. The workman is no longer expected to be in possession of his art; "art" and "work" are distinct, even opposed, orders of making. Moreover, "art" becomes a snob value and the word "art" actually comes to denote the objects that comprise this artificially isolated category of things whose value is maintained in the interests of social prestige. Indeed, the modern world speaks of "art" instead of "works *of* art" because this artificial isolation makes it necessary to distinguish "art" from "non-art" in the category of things made. All this Gill called "art nonsense" and he sought to debunk it in so far as it makes a "false mysticism" of man's creative spirit and distorts the proper order and status of intelligent workmanship.

Gill's indebtedness to the English tradition of radical thought, whose roots go back beyond William Cobbett to Blake and reach forward through Carlyle, Ruskin, Morris, and on to his contemporaries and friends W. R. Lethaby and Edward Johnston, has always been acknowledged. Indeed, Gill's critique of the modern industrial world and his re-affirmation of the dignity of human labor must be set against the perspective of such thought, as his achievement must be seen to be cumulative in respect of their example.

Gill always acknowledged a degree of kinship with William Blake, though he was far from sharing Blake's visionary sense of the imagination. But just as Blake was the prophet of the then industrializing English nation, so Gill may yet be seen as the prophet of post-industrial England. Blake was an artisan engraver in late eighteenth-century London, a time of decline in many such trades. The influx of population drifting away from agricultural subsistence in the fields and villages of rural England had come to form the mass of dispossessed and unskilled proletariat of the new centers of mechanical production. In the wake of this upheaval came the erosion of craft skills, and to Blake this fact highlighted the destructiveness inherent in the process of mechanization. Blake saw this process not indeed primarily as destroying muscle and bone (though it did that well enough) but as destructive of the inner man—*homo faber*—the "Poetic Genius" in every man. "A Machine is not a Man nor Work of Art; it is destructive of Humanity & of Art", he declared in his *Public Address* of 1810. He had already, in about 1788, in his two tracts *There is no Natural Religion* and *All Religions are One*, found it necessary to point out that the nature of man is Infinite, in opposition to the encroaching philosophies of the mechanic system based exclusively upon a knowledge derived wholly from the bodily organs of perception. Such a bounded universe, as he saw, would be "loathed by its possessor", for in denying man the Infinite that is connatural to him it binds him to the Ratio merely of his own ego.

In these tracts Blake settles once and for all the terms of reference for the ensuing radical debate on the destructiveness of the mechanical system. When Gill claimed, in his *The Necessity of Belief*, that "death is the actual aim of industrialism, its diabolic direction", it was nothing new. Blake had seen it a century earlier and had spoken out against it in a powerful passage in his Jerusalem:

> all the Arts of Life they chang'd into the Arts of Death in Albion.
> The hour-glass contemn'd because its simple workmanship
> Was like the workmanship of the plowman, & the water wheel
> That raises water into cisterns, broken & burn'd with fire
> Because its workmanship was like the workmanship of the shepherd;
> And in their stead, intricate wheels invented, wheel without wheel,
> To perplex youth in their outgoings & to bind to labors in Albion
> Of day & night the myriads of eternity; that they may grind
> And polish brass & iron hour after hour, laborious task,

> Kept ignorant of its use: that they might spend the days of
> wisdom
> In sorrowful drudgery to obtain a scanty pittance of bread,
> In ignorance to view a small portion & think that All,
> And call it Demonstration, blind to all the simple rules of
> life.

This passage anticipates a good deal of the thought Gill expressed a century later after the same system had consistently proven its social and human divisiveness as well as its spiritual impotence.

Cobbett rode on horseback over the southern counties of the same England that Blake knew. A prodigious worker himself, Cobbett knew the importance to a just society of a right and responsible livelihood for its people. He witnessed the rural aspect of the social upheaval created by the drift of population to the "Great Wen".[2] For him its effect was not only social but was recognizable in the fact that it laid waste the land. Cobbett had a hatred of unproductive land. For him, where beauty and utility had been put asunder there could be no natural beauty in a situation that was morally unacceptable. He poured his inimitable scorn on those responsible for the enclosure of the common land. The consequent lack of ownership of the means of subsistence meant that the dispossessed agricultural laborer was as much the slave of the "Lords of the Loom" as was the factory worker. Cobbett saw, and knew that he saw, the germinating seeds of the modern consumer society. His denunciation of the increasing self-sufficiency of the body of "idlers and traffickers" who create the modern market place, keeping apart those who produce things and those who have need of them, had its basis in the observation that, in such conditions, both the producer and the consumer must gradually relinquish control over the means of production in favor of the "middle-men, who create nothing, who add to the value of nothing, who improve nothing . . . and who live well, too, out of the labor of the producer and the consumer". Cobbett was no less aware of the effect of all this upon the mass of city slaves. Here his analysis of the "calamity" occasioned by the mechanic inven-

---

[2] This was Cobbett's term for the spreading metropolis of London and its growing mercantile power.

tion prefigures Gill's concern that the machine is only acceptable if wholly owned and directed by the worker himself who must also have the benefit of the profits that accrue to its working: "We must have the machine *at home* and we ourselves must have the *profit* of it; for, if the machine be *elsewhere*; if it be worked *by other hands*; if *other persons* have the *profit* of it . . . then the machine is an injury to us", he wrote in his *Rural Rides*.

Beyond recognizing the dignity it may lend, and the injustice, when its fruits are withheld, that labor may occasion man, Cobbett said little about the inherent nature of work. But Thomas Carlyle went further. In the chapter "Labor", in his *Past and Present*, he saw that "there is a perennial nobleness, and even sacredness in work". Moreover, "a man perfects himself by working", for "even in the meanest sorts of Labor, the whole soul of a man is composed into a kind of real harmony".

Carlyle saw into the center of the active life of the working man. Recognizing a sort of Platonic justice there, he wrote, "Blessed is he who has found his work" for in "the inmost heart of the Worker rises a god-given Force". For him the only knowledge is that which holds good in working—the rest is "hypothesis of knowledge". In such thoughts Carlyle comes close to expressing the traditional notion of the marriage of wisdom and method in all vocational endeavor—"Admirable is that of the old Monks, '*Laborare est Orare*, Work is Worship'"—a balance of the contemplative and active life, of the intelligence and the will, the harmony of reposed soul and dynamic body. In Carlyle we have a foretaste of Gill's thought that as man is the summit of nature, so his art improves on nature, and that every man is a special kind of artist. In the same work Carlyle wrote, "He that works, whatsoever be his work, he bodies forth the form of Things Unseen; a small Poet every Worker is". The humblest platter, the Epic Poem, these that Nature has not yet seen he creates—to Her a "No-thing!"—these the worker summons from the Unseen, "in and for the Unseen". He who looks to the powers of this world must ever play at the deceiving of his true self—the unspeaking voice of conscience, the silent reverberation of perfection in his nature. The worker who, for whatever reason, looks to "the world and its wages", works at a "Sham-thing" which is best not done. Thus Carlyle saw, before Ruskin, that the tragedy of industrial work, "under bondage to Mammon", was the enforced idleness of "the rational soul" it induced in the worker, stopping the springs of charity and thus destroying the moral basis of human intercourse.

If the ultimate nature of Carlyle's religious notions was somewhat vague, there was no mistaking the "true Deity" of his age: "Mechanism". Under this secular god men no longer feel the pull of the "internal perfection"; their faith, as he wrote in his essay, "Signs of the Times", is "for external combinations and arrangements, for institutions, constitutions,—for Mechanism of one sort or other, do they hope and struggle. Their whole efforts, attachments, opinions, turn on mechanism, and are of a mechanical character."

The well-springs of faith in the "Deity of Mechanism" had been pinpointed by Coleridge in his *Statesman's Manual* of 1816, some 13 years before the prophetic text of Carlyle's essay. The "mechanic philosophy", Coleridge wrote (elaborating on Blake's tracts, as it were), "demanding for every mode and act of existence real or possible visibility, knows only of distance and nearness, composition (or rather juxtaposition) and decomposition, in short the relation of unproductive particles to each other; so that in every instance the result is the exact sum of the component quantities, as in arithmetical addition. This is the philosophy of death, and only of a dead nature can it hold good." This "philosophy of death", founded on the mechanism of Hobbes, the empiricism of Locke, and the economics of Adam Smith, had issued in a

> commercial spirit, and the ascendancy of the experimental philosophy which . . . combined to foster its [the discursive understanding's] corruption. Flattered and dazzled by the real or supposed discoveries, which it had made, the more the understanding was enriched, the more did it become debased; till science itself put on a selfish and sensual character, and immediate utility, in exclusive reference to the gratification of the wants and appetites of the animal, the vanities and caprices of the social, and the ambition of the political, man was imposed as the test of all intellectual powers and pursuits. Worth was degraded in to a lazy synonym of value; and value was exclusively attached to the interest of the senses.

Carlyle, in his moment of vision in "Signs of the Times", caught an echo of the warning sounded by Coleridge: that the mechanical model by which men hoped to shape the world shapes man in its turn. Men come to conceive and understand themselves on the model of external circumstances. Cultivated on exclusively mechanical principles, the inward is finally abandoned and the mind is emptied of any significance other than that of evincing the mechanical method. This undue cultivation of the outward overrides and considers as nothing the "Dynamic", as Carlyle called it, in man's nature: "the primary, unmodified forces and energies of man, the mysterious springs of Love, and Fear, and Wonder, of Enthusiasm, Poetry, Religion, all which have a truly vital and infinite character." More and more, development comes to mean something external and measurable; social virtues are equated with political and economic expediency. "Men are to be guided only by their self-interests." The cash nexus that binds the worker to his employer becomes the standard by which men measure all effort and reward. When the sufficiency and corruption of public laws prove their inability to maintain an effective balance of "self-interests"—for it is the law of the new political economy that property should be concentrated and protected—exploitation comes as naturally as fruit to the tree.

With regard to the ethical neutrality of a system of manufacture in which work had atrophied to a mere mechanical function, Ruskin (as Gill acknowledged in his essay devoted to him) saw "clearly that the roots of human action, and therefore of human art, are moral roots". Just as, in the face of the rapid advance of the new system, Carlyle had found it necessary to point to the contrast between the "Dynamical" and the "Mechanic" Method, so Ruskin in his turn points to the moral contrast in the division of society inimical to the "Mercantile Economy"; the economy of "pay" signifies the legal, moral, and social claims made by the few upon the labor of the many: poverty and debt on the one side, riches and right on the other. But for one who had seen that "there is no wealth but life" the iniquities of the disproportion in reward between employer and employed were less important than those of a system that could manufacture anything "except men". It was not so much the division of labor or the "degradation of the operative into a machine" that the system had achieved, but the division of men themselves, "broken into small fragments and crumbs of life", as he put it in *The Stones of Venice.*

Like Carlyle before him and Coomaraswamy and Gill a century later, Ruskin had glimpsed the truth that every man was a special kind of artist and thought the task of the reformer was to rekindle in every laborer that "power for better things", the "*thoughtful* part" of him which must be prized and honored even in its imperfection "above the best and most perfect manual skill" such as the mechanic system produces. This way he would be "made a man", whereas by the "mechanic" system he had been reduced to a mere "animated tool". In *Unto This Last* Ruskin had castigated his uncomprehending contemporaries for their unquestioning reliance upon the modern political economy itself built upon the premises of Mill, Malthus, Ricardo, etc. What the new science had left out of account was precisely the "motive power of the soul". It was this very unacknowledged quality, the soul, that seeped into every quantitative calculation of the "political economist's equations, without his knowledge, and falsifies every one of their results". Work is best done, not for pay or under pressure but "only when the motive force, that is to say, the will or spirit of the creature, is brought to its greatest strength" by the "social affections"—precisely what the political economist is likely to see as merely "accidental and disturbing elements in human nature". Blake, Coleridge, Carlyle, and then Ruskin, each struggled to keep open a sense of the soul's worth in the face of its gradual occlusion by the closed system that accepts as its sole province the domain of what can be measured and weighed.

But Ruskin, though he had seen that the work of mere utility—the "dishonor of manual labor"—must be done away with altogether, showed the impotence with which Gill charged him when it came to the question of the beautiful. With the eye of an aesthete whose vision is formed on an inverted materialism, he wrote in *Modern Painters*: "Any material object which can give us pleasure in the simple contemplation of its outward qualities without any direct or definite exertion of the intellect, I call in some way, or in some degree, beautiful." For Ruskin the beautiful was always something incidental, something added, like a sheen or gloss to the being of a thing, not a light within it.

Never a cognitive principle, beauty is always, for Ruskin, an affective impulse and is sensational as to its object. It is thus not surprising that "art", far from being the rational principle of normal workmanship, was not much more for him than whatever elicits his deepest feelings at delighted observation—and the artist, one who can depict such feelings. Attempting to unite beauty and workmanship, in a passage in *The Two Paths*, he wrote: "Beautiful art can only be produced by people who have beautiful things about them, and leisure to look at them; and unless you provide some elements of beauty for your workmen to be surrounded by, you will find that no elements of beauty can be invented by them."

William Morris' wrestling with the divisive monster of beauty on the one hand and utility on the other took a different form yet again from that of his predecessors. He saw through the fallacy of the Protestant ethic—used as an expedient to bridge the divide—that work, any work, because it serves "the sacred cause of labor", is good in itself. This same fallacy Carlyle had come close to advocating. For Morris, the evil shadow of the industrial system obscured the light of an obvious truth: there are, he wrote in *Useful Work Versus Useless Toil*, "two kinds of work: one good, the other bad; one not far removed from a blessing, a lightening of life; the other a mere curse, a burden to life". The work it was manly to do has hope in it, a threefold hope—"hope of rest, hope of product, hope of pleasure in the work itself". All other work "is slave's work mere toiling to live, that we may live to toil". Such was the heritage of the dispossessed peasants of the eighteenth century who became the proletariat of the nineteenth. Such facts remained fundamental to Gill's view of contemporary society. He too saw that the tyranny of the modern market place consists in the fact that the buyer, far from being an enlightened patron (which he could still in a measure be at the country fairs Cobbett saw must be destroyed by the increased trafficking of middlemen in shops), is no more in possession of an educated taste and discretion that any other consumer of those goods which are called into existence for no other reason than to serve as the very life-blood of the system of their production. For Morris the smart of injustice was in the enforced degradation of man at this "tax of waste", this treadmill futility that is a trading on the ignorance of the productive masses by the profit-gathering minority who have "the power of compelling other men to work against their will". For Gill (who transposed many of Morris' observations into the terms of his own philosophy), no less than for Morris, this imposition upon the worker to labor against his will was by necessity inherent in the mechanical system; the necessity to destroy in the worker any real intellectual responsibility he might have for what he makes. As Morris put it in *How We Live and How We Might Live*: "they do not know what they are working at, nor whom they are working for, because they are combining to produce wares of which the profit of a master forms an essential part, instead of goods for their own use." Moreover, "they will be in fact just a part of the machinery for the production of profit; and so long as this lasts it will be the aim of the masters or profit-makers to decrease the market value of this human part of the machinery." This is easily recognizable as the foundation of Gill's mature view of the question of the modern worker being merely the sentient part of the machine who has only his energies with which to trade his life and whose life must be put at its lowest acceptable value by his masters.

In seeking a solution to the redistribution of justice as well as profit, like Ruskin before him, Morris was to founder on the rock of beauty, which was for him a subjective addition to life and its necessary utilities. Hence, as Morris supposed, if the worker is freed from the iniquities of a system that encroaches at every moment upon his work and his leisure time as well as his artistic and his moral accountability, he would make things at a sufficient pace of leisure that the work of his hands (it would come to this), in harmony with his pleasure at creation, would add beauty to his products. Thus would come about the "pleasant life", a sort of paradise on Earth whose occupants would have: "First, a healthy body; second, an active mind in sympathy with the past, the present, and the future; thirdly, occupation fit for a healthy body and an active mind; fourthly, a beautiful world to live in."

Given Gill's integrated religious and metaphysical viewpoint, it was inevitable that he would come to reject this vaguely humanist dream of a paradise whose *raison d'être* is curiously absent: inevitable that he should see that Morris' politics were those of time and not of eternity. Gill, in judging Morris, applied the same principle as on so many occasions and went straight to the heart of the matter: "He saw no being behind doing." Morris' predominant concern was for the fact that, by the mechanical system, the workman is robbed of the pleasure and satisfaction of free creative effort, and a just reward for his labor. But Gill's concern was for the fact that the worker, in being robbed of intellectual responsibility, is also robbed of the possibility of apprehending the holiness of the creation and of his own being by means of a life of work as prayer; a norm of manufacture connatural to man's rational intelligence. Even though he was prepared to concede that art cannot flourish in the hands of a coterie of specially gifted men, Morris none the less thought that art must be the outcome of a vaguely humanistic aspiration towards what he called the "beauty and true pleasure of life". Despite his undoubted personal mastery of the many crafts he practiced, Morris had no proper doctrine of work. When he came to describe his vision of the social revolution he had called for—which revolution was no more than "a stage of the great journey of evolution that joins the future and the past to the present"—we find that vision trailing off into an increasingly attenuated generalization: "I console myself with visions of the noble communal hall of the future, unsparing of materials, generous in worthy ornament, alive with the noblest thoughts of our time, and the past, embodied in the best art which a free and manly people could produce." The artist's role in the construction of such a society was to produce no more than "beauty and interest".

It is significant that both Ruskin and Morris believed that greater leisure and a higher standard of living would lead to the restitution of the arts among the people. By contrast Gill called for a "holy poverty" as the only rational attitude to material things; hence his criticism of Morris that "he saw joy in labor but no sacrifice". What is more, Gill foresaw that in the Welfare State the "factory hand" would come to despise the culture of "higher things" for which he is supposedly made free by the mechanical system. How right he was!

Although he had learned much from Morris, Gill rejected him. It was as much a rejection of the Arts and Crafts movement as a whole as of Morris himself. Gill also rejected the socialism that went with their vision on the grounds that they had no effective answer to the system they affected to despise; a system which perpetuated the moral irresponsibility of the capitalist investor on the one hand and the intellectual irresponsibility of the worker on the other. The Arts and Crafts movement had merely established a vogue among the rich for sentimentalism. Socialism had failed to see anything wrong in the industrial system of production as a solution to the problem of human need. As a political movement, therefore, and as Gill observed in his *Autobiography*, it was "hardly more than an attempt to re-order the distribution of factory products and factory profits".

Of this failure of socialism it fell to Morris' disciple W. R. Lethaby to make the obvious point. Now that the conditions of labor had been bettered by the rise of Trade Union power—and seeing that mechanized production cannot form a sufficient basis for human conduct—the task of the Unions must be to attend to the "element of quality in workmanship". Indeed: "As work is the first necessity of existence, the very center of gravity of our moral system, so a proper recognition of work is a necessary basis for all right religion, art, and civilization. Society becomes diseased in direct ratio to its neglect and contempt of labor." Like Carlyle, Ruskin, and Morris, Lethaby too looked for his bearings to the unified tradition of art and workmanship that was the natural expression of the mind of the Middle Ages: "The most distinctive characteristic of the Middle Ages was the honorable position in the State then taken up by labor."

But Lethaby went one step further along the road uniting beauty and use, art and work, by being more explicit and concrete in his definitions. In Lethaby we find a good many of Gill's mature conclusions on the nature of beauty, art, and workmanship, in a verbal form that is close to Gill's own. Indeed, it was Lethaby who wrote in his book on architecture: "we need not trouble about beauty, for that would take care of itself." Among his papers on Art and Labor (published in 1922 as *Form in Civilization*), are aphoristic distillations of thought that might almost have come from Gill's pen: "Beauty is that which when seen we should love"; "Beauty is the 'substance' of things done"; "Beauty is the flowering of labor and service"; "Beauty has to come by the way"; "Appreciation of Beauty should be one with our judgment of essential quality. . . . The sense of Beauty is the work-conscience".

For Lethaby, art is "the right way of doing right things". Art is "ordinary manipulative skill". It is "service before it is delight; it is labor as well as emotion; it is substance as well as expression". "A work of art implies workmanship." "What I mean by art, then, is not the affair of a few but of everybody."

Like Gill, Lethaby, theoretically at least, fused yet did not confuse art and utility. He was fully aware of the transcendental origins of human workmanship and had written widely on themes of myth, symbol, and cult related to what he called in his essay, "The Center of Gravity", "the 'revelation' of the crafts to men". Gill, during his formative years, had been closely associated with Lethaby and would obviously have absorbed much of his teaching. Yet for all the similarity of Lethaby's final position to that of Gill in the theory of beauty, art, and workmanship, there remains the feeling that it is just that: theory. We cannot find anything like the same degree of personal, manipulative, as well as theoretic integrity in Lethaby that we find in the life and work of Gill. Although Lethaby could situate the proper place of beauty in art, art in workmanship and service, he lacks Gill's depth of resonance and conviction in being able to inter-relate spirit and matter, being and doing, man and society, art and utility, beauty and holiness, to an adequate metaphysical structure. And this reservation could apply equally well to all but Blake of those precursors of Gill that we have examined. But to the list of Gill's masters there is one more name to be added. In some ways it is the most important.

It was the mastery of Edward Johnston's calligraphy that first gave Gill a direct experience of what was meant by work conceived and executed out of the living unity of beauty and utility. The excitement of the experience was, he wrote, "as of the intelligence discovering the good . . . and finding it desirable". In his *Autobiography* Gill described the aesthetic "shock" at first seeing Johnston's writing. It transported the younger man: "I was caught unprepared. I did not know such beauties could exist. I was struck as by lightning, as by a sort of enlightenment: . . . and for a brief second seemed to know even as God knows."

Much of what Gill himself was to absorb from Johnston's teaching remained axiomatic: *making* refers to the material object, *doing* to action and intention; the worker is one who works in substances, and these substances demand a special method. Thus the substance impinges directly upon the form of the thing to be made. The worker thinks of substance, object, and design as inseparable factors in the process of workmanship. The product of work is substance brought to life—and that which is thus brought to life is the very mark of the worker's being. The primary occasion of work is use. Good work is fit purpose. Use and purpose determine the proper treatment of the object. The worker aims at beauty only indirectly as attaining a measure of divine reward. Use and beauty define the axis of embodied truth—usefulness being the end most immediately and commonly apprehended. It is use that curbs the three sins to which the workman is prey: lack of resolve, meaningless imitation, and affectation. Such thoughts of Johnston's, learned as the practical wisdom of human facture, lasted Gill all his life.

In an important passage in his *Autobiography* Gill makes a confession and in so doing makes an important and fundamental distinction, one that helps us to understand the complex process of absorption and rejection in his approach to his masters: "my socialism was from the beginning a revolt against the intellectual degradation of the factory hands and the damned ugliness of all that capitalist industrialism produced, and it was not primarily a revolt against the cruelty and injustice of the possessing classes or against the misery of the poor. It was not so much the working *class* that concerned me as the working *man*—not so much what he got *from* working as what he did *by* working." Thus, for all their concern at the social injustice of the mechanized system, for all that they had shown themselves sensitive to the archetype of beauty, arguing for its return at the heart of human labor in the face of the increasing dehumanization of mechanical production, Gill's precursors had not got to the root of the matter. They had not questioned consistently, deeply, and vigorously enough the nature of man's being.

It is Gill's insistence on starting nearly every argument with the implied question "What is Man?" and following up with penetrating clarity its necessary and rational corollaries that distinguish him from his masters. In recovering the norm of human workmanship on the basis of the whole meaning of life, Gill avoided the fallacy (one to which modern man is particularly prone) of attempting to establish the criteria for the active life in the productive outcome of the active life itself. The depth and conviction of Gill's achievement is present in virtue of his total response to the truth of those metaphysical doctrines he made his own but which were no less the possession of the perennial wisdom that at nearly all times and places has been the normal spiritual legacy of man.

What of Eric Gill today? It would be all too easy to dismiss him as a nostalgic reactionary who, in looking back to the ideals of an earlier age, placed himself out of court in so far as the problems of late twentieth-century society are concerned. But such a judgment would not only be superficial, it would also be wrong. Gill, by the absolute categories of his thought and by his constant appeal to reason placed himself at the center of things. The problems that engaged his mind are still with us. Far from being resolved, they have merely been brought, in the years since his death, to a new level of sophistry, becoming an unquestioned part of the social and intellectual malaise. Time and again Gill thinks his way to the root of those fallacies and contradictions upon which modern society unwittingly rests: its social and productive system that has the incentive of "plenty" linked to mass leisure as one of its implied aims, yet which leads to little more than a disenchanted consumerism; its sentimentalizing of art while dehumanizing work; its pursuit of individualism by means that tend to even greater conformity and standardization; its denial of the place and significance of the Infinite in a world expected to yield "infinite" material development. Only those who have capitulated to the premises on which the current social and economic condition of society rests can afford the specious luxury of seeing Gill as an outmoded figure.

There is now a growing body of opinion that would hold that if the industrialized world is to recover its balance it can only do so on the basis of a re-sacralization of work such as Gill points to. A system of production, fuelled by a morally neutral capital investment that in turn fuels a technological development which is itself blind in so far as the ultimate goal of society is concerned, can give only the appearance of justice (in improved conditions, higher salaries, etc.) not the reality of it. The driving force of such a society, Gill saw, can lend nothing to a vision of that final end from which man must take the meaning of his existence. If the industrial system frees man for "higher things" by reducing his need to labor, why must there be such an outcry at the consequences of paid unemployment? As Gill observed in his little essay "Slavery and Freedom", slavery may no more be necessarily uncomfortable than freedom comfortable.

Gill's views on economics and politics have been criticized as being naive, presumably by those who would consider the economics of industrial production—with its insatiable appetite for the Earth's resources, not to mention the attendant problems of wide-scale dereliction and pollution—enlightened. Simple and unaffected his views may have been, but never as if unacquainted with evil. Hence, in his observation that "machinery . . . does not, in fact, exist to make things at all [but] to make the thing called profits" is foreshadowed the observation that the modern economy is primarily concerned to produce demand. In seeing the man of business as being at the mercy of "undisciplined fancies", Gill recognized the remorseless circularity of that unique form of modern slavery, "consumerism". He saw that its victim, the "consumer"—that final triumph of "economic man"—has no choice but to roam the market place in order to squander the "fee" paid him for the time spent supporting a system whose very existence depends upon contriving ways to stimulate a demand for goods that can never wholly satisfy that demand. Such is the treadmill of "consumer choice" and hence it comes about that men must serve "the Economy" for the good of a society that has no higher notion of the social good than that of "free enterprise" serving consumer demand. Already, in *News from Nowhere*, Morris had spoken of the inevitable downward spiral whereby "the production of measureless quantities of worthless makeshifts" knew no limit since "the only admitted test of utility in wares was the finding of buyers for them—wise men or fools, as it might chance." Producer and consumer alike, must come to suffer the smart of tyranny when "the Economy" has the power of Holy Writ!

In the field of "art", too, in so far as it is a separate and specialized domain of activity in modern society, Gill's views are no less timely. By insisting on the connatural nature of common sensibility and pure being in the intuition of beauty, Gill effectively joined what had for some centuries been artificially separated: Being and knowing, loving and thinking, living and making. His assimilation of beauty to truth and goodness, moreover, provides a path between the twin heresies of post-renaissance aesthetics. The first heresy was the seemingly irreversible persuasion of some four hundred years during which "art" had taken the imitation of appearances as a yardstick for expression. The invention of photography "killed" this heresy, but the counter-measure of the modern movement—an emphasis on the abstract nature of aesthetic values—opened up an equal and opposite heresy. The heresy of naturalism falsifies the nature of reality by tending to limit it to appearances, forgetting that, logically, appearances are of something. The heresy of abstraction falsifies the nature of intelligence in supposing that reality is all in the delight the mind feels in its own correspondence to certain values of pattern and symmetry. It is perhaps not too difficult to see that behind these twin heresies are two equally partial and unconscious theories of the beautiful—at their crudest, the one exclusively objective and the other exclusively subjective. In the objective view beauty is thought to reside in the appearance of the things we perceive. In the subjective view the objective reality of the thing perceived is granted but beauty is thought to belong to the act of emotive assimilation. The objective view will not accept that the act of perception is adaptive and contributory in the assimilation of beauty, while the subjective view will not accept that beauty is not wholly attributable to emotive response. In other words, neither view can accept that beauty is in the order of being. Both forms of heresy tend to overlook the fact that the relationship between mind and beauty—utilizing the simultaneous co-opera-tion of both perception and emotion—is ultimately cognitive and depends more upon the action of the intellect than upon sensory stimulus. "That which is beautiful pleases when seen, and it is the mind which sees and is pleased", Gill wrote in an Appendix to his *Beauty Looks After Herself.* Here and in his essay of the same title he explored the theme in some detail.

On the basis of Gill's doctrine we might notice how it is hardly a coincidence that in a society which unwittingly subscribes to the notion of art as the province of a special sort of person concerned with beauty, art eventually becomes that hypertrophied banality and crudity with which we are all too familiar. Indeed, a society which unconsciously holds that the pursuit of beauty is the purpose of "art" results in an environment unsurpassed in its dehumanizing ugliness; similarly, the pursuit of leisure as the basis of the good life results in a society in which few people find the time to make what is pleasing to our innate sense of what conforms to a good life.

There can be no mistaking the directional impulse of Gill's thought; it is heavenward. Not so much a heaven "up there" as one with a more local habitation: the kingdom of heaven within, which is the kingdom proper to man—that is, to man the maker.

5

Of Art and Skill

Plato, in stating in the *Gorgias* that he could not fairly give the name "art" to anything irrational, was no more than restating a teaching of Pythagoras who is said to have taught that "art" is a habit of co-operating with reason. Aristotle, in his *Nicomachean Ethics*, extended the same line of thought in teaching that "art" is a capacity to make, involving a true course of reason. This doctrine makes it clear that the creative principle that is art is a rational habit or disposition of the mind to pursue a true course of action in making something. Thus, art stays inside the artist, being understood in terms of the imposition of form upon substance or matter—sound if he is composer, stone if a mason, and so on. But at a higher level it was understood as an analogue of a cosmic principle, whereby the *Logos*, the Divine Reason, manifests itself in the world of created things. The human artist, by imposing order and beauty upon substance, operates in imitation of how God creates the beauty and order of the world, of how He shapes the order of the Creation from the Divine Intellect according to the cosmic possibilities that properly belong to it and thereby perfect its manifestation.

The teaching that "art" is intimately wedded to reason and rationality was propounded through the centuries in one formulation or another until the Scholastic masters of the Middle Ages. St. Bonaventure's *Retracing the Arts to Theology* was perhaps the last extended treatise to expound the doctrine of art, or making according to skill, as a type of rational wisdom that imitates, ultimately a divine prototype. But that was then. We live now in different times. Few people today who think of themselves as artists would instinctively associate the practice of their art as being due to a habit of reason that has a cosmic significance.

We can hardly doubt that art, in our time, is widely thought of as something added to life, an optional extra, a diversion practiced by specialists whose products somehow transcend the more mundane requirements needed to sustain our material and economic existence. We are aware that, as if to counter this situation, it is often hinted (at least) that a degree of aesthetic gratification is a necessary part of maintaining our psychological health. This argument sometimes carries with it a tacit denial that such gratification was available to less sophisticated cultures than our own. And this despite the fact that our museums and cultural heritage sites present abundant evidence that culture, belief, vocation, livelihood, beauty, and utility were for these cultures unified to a degree that for us is clearly impossible.

Progressively, since the Renaissance, and as a result of the catastrophic divorce of beauty and utility, art has been both understood and practiced in terms of freely exercising a spirit of individual creativity. Indeed, we have perhaps pursued to its limit the idea that art is the expression of an autonomous principle of creativity owing little or nothing to the demands of reason and intelligibility. But this is all part and parcel of a trend in our time in which every idea seems destined to be tested to point of destruction. We have done this with the idea of art. But we have not cleared away the detritus of what remains. We go on with the practice of art assuming that a meaningful and coherent philosophy underwrites whatever is done in art's name. While at best we are in agreement that art is necessary and desirable, at worst much of what is currently presented as art, if our more *avant-garde* music concerts and art exhibitions are anything to go by, is little more than a pathology of irrational and abnormal behavior. No doubt this state of affairs has come about under the suasion of a tyranny that urges innovation in defiance of all meaningful criteria.

We have allowed ourselves to become habituated to using the term "artist" to denote one who creates works of art, but without giving much thought to what is intrinsic to the notion of artistry. Instead, we have drifted along with the vague assumption that the word "artist" designates a person of exceptional, aesthetic sensibility; and that whatever someone who possesses such a sensibility conceives and executes must be the thing we are obliged to call "art". But such an assumption will not stand up to scrutiny. Firstly, and most obviously, it makes it impossible to determine who, justifiably, can be said to possess the defining sensibility that is the mark of the artist in distinction from the broad range of people who are not thought to be artists but who none the less possess and exercise some measure of aesthetic sensibility in their work. Secondly, and interconnected with this shortcoming, the assumption does not allow for a definition of art itself as distinct from the outcome of any other act of making. These two primary weaknesses grow from the now ingrained acceptance of the idea of art as designating, exclusively, a category of external objects or productions having an aesthetic *raison d'être* of their own purely on account of the creator's special sensibility. In this view, quintessentially, art is something external to the artist, having been transferred to the object by an acquiescent consent that art is whatever it is that creative artists do. This further assumption gives rise to a widespread and pressing need to answer the question "What is art?"—a question that so readily comes to the surface in almost any current discussion or appraisal of works of contemporary art. This need is felt alike by the expert no less than by the inexpert.

A change in the way in which we think about art would therefore be timely. To this end we could do no better than return to the traditional and universal understanding of art,[1] one that is more faithful to both the nature and function of art itself, as well as to the wider role it plays in the order and maintenance of civilized society. This would mean that whenever we think of art or refer to an artist we ought to make a mental note that the word "artist" refers to one who is a skilled maker and that art itself is the perfection of work. Aided by this habit we would be re-minded on each occasion of the primary meaning of the word "art".

Our word "art" comes from the Latin *ars*, "a fitting together". *Ars* also designates "skill" and "craft". Our word "skill" has come down from the Middle English "skile", meaning "discernment"/ "judgment". We would do well to re-mind ourselves also that such terms as "artistry", "work", "craft", "masterpiece", "vocation", and "talent" all inescapably imply the sense of a mastery of means applied to a given end: an appropriate and just application

---

[1] See the author's *Every Man An Artist: Readings in the Traditional Philosophy of Art* (Bloomington, IN: World Wisdom, 2005), which, with its Bibliography, might serve as an introduction to this wide-ranging subject.

of a wisdom that is at once of the mind and of the body to a given, intelligible, and practical end.

To the extent that there is any confusion as to what is meant by the word "art", that confusion arises from the fact that our use of that term has, as it were, come adrift from its moorings in this primary sense of being the deployment of a faculty that is as much to do with how we think—how we apply the mind—as it has to do with what we apply it to. All too often the intrinsic, time-honored resonances that are implicit in the notion of art as a skill in predisposing the mind to work fruitfully with reason, are absent from our understanding of what art is. This being so we might venture to recover some of these resonances by examining in more detail what is implicit in the notion of skill itself.

To speak of skill is to speak necessarily of something that is exercised in being applied to something other. Skill cannot be exercised in isolation from something that is thereby altered for the better by its application. The change made by the application of skill comes about in some mode or manner according to both the receptivity and resistance of the other. Skill can no more be exercised in the face of total resistance than it would be needed where its application could produce no effect or gain. Therefore, to speak of skill is to recognize a greater or lesser degree of mastery. Such mastery must be present in the one who exercises skill as well as evident in that to which skill has been applied. This in turn means that both that which applies (mental and bodily effort) and that which is applied (intelligible and practical command) face some inherent opposition in the circumstances that require the exercise of skill. In addition it must be recognized that mental irresolution, physical infirmity, and intellectual confusion, as well as the frequent intractability of whatever skill is applied to, all contribute to the conditions under which skill is directed to overcome this opposition.

To be skilled is more and greater than to be unskilled in an order of values established by convention and precedent in any field of applied skill. It is naturally unjust to value and reward unskilled work over and above skilled work. This is due to our innate recognition that skill, in being applied, must in some measure envisage a given result that cannot be achieved without the proper exercise of skill. It is not the moral worth of the desirable end that is in question here, for skill in itself is concerned only with the good of its exercise, not with the good of the end to which it is applied. A just valuation of skill is due because the exercise of skill facilitates the achievement of a given end, not the desirability of the end itself—the production of an efficient murder weapon, for instance. Where would be the justice in rewarding what thwarts a desired end over and above what facilitates it? This principle of just valuation is as true of the skill of the murderer and the maker of chairs as it is of the philosopher.

The implication of all this is that a degree of knowledge and discernment must be possessed by anyone who wishes to exercise skill and that that knowledge and discernment involve a fuller grasp of reality than would exist if that knowledge and discernment were absent. It would be contrary to, and therefore a perversion of, the nature of intelligence to assign a greater significance and merit to the unskillful than to the skilful in achievements of a like nature.

The final goal of skill implies the perfect integration of conception and execution. This presupposes an effective correspondence between the state of mind of the worker and the circumstances that call for skill's application. These circumstances may themselves be of the mind (there is a skill in the proper application of intelligence), or of the handling of the things that make up the practical and material fabric of life. In both cases precedent and convention form the basis on which the exercise of skill proceeds, even though they are not the necessary criteria for artistic value. Precedent and convention must, however, necessarily form the implicit condition for the exercise of skill. No one sets about applying skill at random with a completely blank mind and in a spirit of total innovation. The aptitude implied by skill presupposes an ability to envisage in the mind appropriate action and effective realization—*what* needs to be done and *how* it can be done. Both are largely cultural acquisitions shaped by past practice and experience. To want always to break with convention (that self-indulgent dream of the *avant-garde*) in the name of a creative spirit that believes that innovation has an absolute right to impose itself upon the making of anything, is to pursue the chimera of a freedom that is quite literally without meaning. It is akin to believing that to give free rein to a spirit of mischief in changing the shapes of the letters of the alphabet *at will* would increase the expressive powers of language. This in turn would be to pretend that we are obliged continually to invent reality rather than, as our possession of intelligence discovers, reality is that to which we must continually align our experience if we are to understand it. It is here, in the complex interweaving of convention, precedent, memory, and imagination, and much else that is necessary to the practice of any art, that we most clearly witness the impoverishment brought about by allowing the idea that the artist is a skilled maker to be eclipsed by the assumption that he or she is a purveyor of aesthetic sensation and idiosyncratic production.

The fact that skill, as a practical wisdom, necessarily depends upon memory and imagination and therefore upon precedent and convention indicates that skill cannot be meaningful independently of a set of values and criteria that make possible agreement as to the merit and relevance of its exercise. That is to say, for skill to be effective there must be a measure of consensus as to the appropriate occasion and conditions for its application. And since skill is something applied to something other than itself the merit of its application cannot inhere in skill itself. To exercise skill for its own sake is to make of means and ends one and the same thing. But, properly, the applied end of skill is determined by the values and criteria that themselves determine the merit of its application. Without these values and criteria there can be no assessment of skill since, in the absence of any distinction between means and ends, there is no way to judge how means have served ends. All of which is to say that the exercise of skill implicitly recognizes a standard against which its application is necessarily evaluated, a standard that is independent of the contingencies that warrant its application.

If the artist, as skilled workman, is not in possession of an appropriate skill, the result is noted as a deficiency. By definition a recognized failure to achieve a result cannot be accounted a greater or more complete accomplishment than failure to achieve the same result. Moreover, recognition of deficiency to achieve an end indicates that a desirable outcome must in some sense be discernible. It implies an evaluation against which the deficiency is proved. This evaluation is the measure of the ratio of intention to result. Without it there can be no recognition of the extent to which skilled application has fallen short of an intention to achieve an end result. Without such an evaluation can any artistic judgment be possible?[2]

The standard by which skill is judged must be held in common by both the maker and the informed patron. (There are many occasions when they will be one and the same.) If it is the skill of the maker to operate effectively towards a given end, then it is the skill of the patron to be able to appraise the outcome of the operation—the effectiveness of the means deployed to achieve a given end. The common end of a skilled operation and a desirable result would not be realizable were the value of skill not present in its application. To deploy skill without any conception of a desirable result would be to assume the autonomous value of each and every exercise of skill, as if there could be no comparison of one skilled application from another in circumstances of a like nature. But this is not how we experience the result of skill, where it is clear that some assessment as between one application and another arises naturally from the conditions of the application itself.

The values and criteria by which a legitimate end may be determined cannot include the arbitrary and the unintelligible. How could skill, by its very nature meant to effect a change towards improvement, be deployed towards that which by definition cannot be foreseen or towards that which is incapable of being understood? This would by no means bar the "happy accident", even if it must be recognized that in so far as the exercise of skill is an acquired faculty, we would not undertake to perfect a faculty in the absence of any understanding of its possible outcome? This is tantamount to recognizing at a human level a truth that is equally applicable at a cosmic level whereby, as Plato states in the *Timaeus*, "everything that becomes or is created must of necessity be created by some cause, for without a cause nothing can be created". In relation to skill, what constitutes a cause is a

---

[2] See A. K. Coomaraswamy's "Intention" in *Selected Papers 1, Traditional Art and Symbolism,* edited by Roger Lipsey (Princeton: Princeton University Press, 1977), pp. 266-75.

desirable end, and this is by no means limited to the production of a physical object or action. Human needs embrace the mind no less than the body. The skilled formulation of a metaphysical or religious truth is as necessary as is the production of the objects that facilitate daily life: "And I have filled him with the spirit of God, in wisdom, and in understanding, and in knowledge, and in all manner of workmanship. . . . And in the hearts of all that are wise hearted I have put wisdom, that they make all that I have commanded thee" (Exodus 31:3, 6).

We live in a time when the nature and merit of art has never before received so much scrutiny. This in turn generates an unprecedented quantity of evaluation and judgment as to the merit and/or greatness (or otherwise) of art and artists. But in the context of a more or less unrestrained freedom of personal creativity being accepted as the ultimate *raison d'être* for the practice of art, no standard (other than a consensus of opinion), nothing outside the act of making itself, permits the distinction of means from ends that must be the foundation of evaluation. For evaluation implies the presence or absence of accomplishment, else what would be the purpose of any evaluation? Is there not obviously a qualitative difference between the exercise of skill and random activity? No supposed artistic judgment pretends to make a valuation on the basis of effort alone. This would be to measure behavior rather than accomplishment. What draws us to a work of art (accomplishment) is not, or should not, be the personality of the artist, but the work's achievement in the context of conventions and precedents already established. There is no shortage of evidence to demonstrate that the tyranny of unrestrained innovation that is supposed to legitimize the spirit of creative freedom has in our time replaced the idea that rational habits of mind are the necessary predisposition for the practice of any work of skill. (To the extent that, for instance, it is now common for "conceptual artists" to exhibit work under their own name which they have not themselves executed.) This change in the way we think about art could have come about only by ignoring the fact that established conventions and precedents must be the implied cause of any attempt to break from or replace them. The creative strategy of an *avant-garde* amounts to moving continuously forward into a judgmental vacuum where criteria and values can have no applicability. In effect it is an attempt to repeatedly wipe clean the slate of past experience and wisdom—never to let it accumulate.

No real and effective assessment of the merit of a work of skilled making can be undertaken where the end to which the means of skill is applied is not in some sense disclosed by the work itself. This fact is as fundamental to any understanding of what has been lost by art when it is practiced in isolation from the normal context of the work and skill that supplies the needs of livelihood. It is also central to the problem we allude to whenever we ask of a work of art we do not recognize as such, "What is it?" We all know what a cup, or a chair, or an icon, or a cathedral is, and are able to re-cognize the value of their kind. In the sphere of the arts this act of cognition requires a generic identity for it to be meaningful. Without this identity we cannot know *what* is intended and all grounds for critical evaluation are thereby undermined. If "creative activity" is exercised without the objectivity generic identity provides, then it is difficult to see how any accomplishment can be measured. What are we to make, for instance, of a room where, simply, the light goes on and off, exhibited as a work of art? Any real and effective standard of art must in some measure be in conformity with past accomplishment and experience. This is no more than a recognition that each thing made by true art has a generic reality; a reality that is disclosed *by* the work of skill itself. No meaningful work of skill is undertaken without some knowledge of this generic reality, just as no art, whether it be that of farming, motherhood, the sculpting of statues, or the making of poems, is practiced on the supposition that the result is never seen, used, or appreciated by someone other than the artist.

In *re*-minding ourselves, then, of the tradition of thinking of art as a skilled making, "involving a true course of reason", we note that it is neither exclusively nor specifically the task of the maker to determine the appropriateness or otherwise of the need that calls for the production of a work of art. But it is specifically the maker's task alone to judge finally the success or otherwise of *how* a thing is made. The appeal to an unqualified and self-governing spirit of "creative freedom", however, cannot help but obscure the interrelation of productive method, accomplishment, and responsibility in the way that it obscures the distinction of means from ends. It is certainly unwise for man to be without all sense of responsibility for the results of his actions in any sphere. But in matters that concern the artist's responsibility for the outcome of his art, this clearly requires a legitimate objectivity in the deployment of means to achieve a given end: an objectivity that must by its very nature rest upon an adequate distinction of means from ends.

To suppose that art is the product of "creative freedom" alone, subjectivizes the richly complex process whereby a work of art comes into being, is comprehended, and valued. It does so by tacitly claiming that it is the inalienable right of the artist to set the terms of the wisdom and discernment that both the practice and understanding of art (skill) demand. But the complexity of this demand cannot do otherwise than accumulate deposits in convention and precedent, the disowning of which, in the name of innovation, is made in the face of the obvious truth that art (skill) is the means to effect an end that cannot be art itself.

Such confusions no doubt feed the current trend whereby artistic assessment and judgment seem to be largely in abeyance. Everything, it seems, has become grist to the mill of the "creative freedom" of the much-vaunted contemporary artist for whom "anything goes". Nothing can fail or be judged to be inadequate in such circumstances. This, in reality, is a state of self-imposed intellectual vacuity in which it is impossible to objectively establish the need, intelligibility, and valuation of the work in question. If the purpose of art is simply to exercise a creative freedom (in effect a license to indulge unintelligibility), then that exercise itself becomes both the means and the end of the experience that is "art". In which case how can what that exercise produces be justifiably offered for objective appraisal? Surely such an exercise would be its own reward regardless of anything incidentally produced in its name?

Nothing that has been said above should be interpreted as arguing that the exercise of skill is sufficient of itself to produce works of artistic quality. The doctrine of art as a discernment that remains in the artist certainly argues that skill is a necessary cause of works of art. It does not argue that it is the sufficient cause. In so far as the doctrine may act as a guide to the wisdom or otherwise of man's making and doing it might be said to guard against the inevitable productive and aesthetic impulses of man being given free rein in isolation from the practical condition of his environment on the one hand, and the integral requirements of his spiritual constitution on the other. For these are the polar axes between which the human state functions normally. The traditional doctrine of art as a pre-formal habit of reason undoubtedly implies that the production of works of art without skill is impossible. It says nothing about skill being an arbiter of taste. Who cannot call to mind many examples of art that exhibit a high degree of applied skill, yet are none the less repellent or perverse? There is, after all, such a thing as virtuosity just as there is decadence. The two are causally linked where skill conveys an impression of superfluity and uselessness. In such cases it can be a question of unintelligence and sentimentality over-playing the expressive means beyond what is sufficient for the formal demands of the production in question. The extravagances of the Baroque are hardly lacking in skill, even as their overweening embellishment suffocates the need for intelligent restraint in the expression of piety. Bad taste has to do with the artist not treating the substance he works with the integral truth due to its qualitative properties: objectively, an abuse of the material substance or subjectively, a perversion of the normal requirements of intelligence and sensibility—the sculptor who strives to make stone simulate as near as possible the sensuous quality of flesh, or the poet who plays upon base sentimentalities to secure the reader's sympathy for instance. Certainly skill is a dimension of the beauty of art since skill is needed to bring a work of art to its formal perfection, which must include the sense of its being fitted exactly to good and appropriate need and use. Excessive skill becomes bad taste precisely when it gives evidence of an element of deception—as we see hinted, albeit distantly, in the word "crafty".

Nothing in the traditional doctrine of art as skill forbids or excludes the possibility, the desirability—even the necessity—of innovation. It certainly denies that innovation is itself the purpose and justification for art, which it does in the context of an understanding that sees innovation as naturally arising out of any particular need to guide the application of skill towards the realization of an idea. But innovation in this case would have no license to do more than what is required to realize the perfection of the idea in question. This integral perfection is not only what is compromised whenever innovation is pursued for its own sake; it is also what is absent from the pursuit of "creative freedom".

6

Thoughts on Reading Frithjof Schuon's
Writings on Art

We live in a time of utmost confusion in which the sense of what is qualitatively essential to life is continuously obscured by an unrestrained quantity, both of ideas and of products. As a result what is often conceived as a means to recover that sense of what is essential only serves as a contribution to further confusion. Given that this confusion is both engendered by and in turn engenders fresh errors, there is an exemplary case for proposing that only arguments based directly on universal truths are adequate to throw light on our unprecedented situation. At the end of a civilization, and by way of recompense for the relative depletion of grace from the cosmic setting, there is both a need and an obligation to overcome the "metaphysical depreciation" incurred by the passage of time by essential summary—a recall to both order and orientation. Only universal truths can satisfy the needs of that condition that is the mental turmoil and spiritual demoralization of modern man. Indeed, one might ask whether the necessity for such a metaphysical perspective is bound to give rise to the articulation of the required truths. The writings of Frithjof Schuon have this providential function.

Any reader, coming across Schuon's writings for the first time, might find themselves nonplussed by the absence in them of what is usually regarded as historical context. For the most part we are accustomed to studying art as a repository of "exhibits" and the part these play in the evolution of cultural history. What is frequently overlooked is that this approach to art surrenders both culture and history to a purely horizontal progression that obscures the value of art. Values are intrinsic to a vertical dimension that links subjective experience of outward forms to the "absolute" objectivity of Beauty, Truth, and Goodness, and all that is inherent in them with respect to the human vocation. Schuon's discussion of art takes all its bearings from this vertical dimension, centered as it is on the integral nature of man's deiformity.

If we were to ask what might be a possible precedent for these writings,[1] we could, with appropriate reservations, point to the example of Ananda K. Coomaraswamy. Certainly Coomaraswamy was the first scholar to propound universal criteria of art based on the study of its conceptions and practices in both East and West. His scholarly brilliance was put to the study of the metaphysical, doctrinal, and practical evidence for the conclusions he arrived at. The prodigious range of his scholarly grasp and the depth of his penetration into the meaning of the texts and works of art he studied, was presented by him as the "theoretic" evidence of a truth one might choose to deviate from but which one could not confute, being as it is part of a body of wisdom that has a "self-authenticating intelligibility". This observation is not meant to illustrate anything other than that in Coomaraswamy's writings there is less the sense of a being living at the heart of the doctrines he expounded and more the sense of a mind of almost superhuman concentration and concision whose whole effort is to demonstrate truth by means of what, at its most extreme, one might call a sort of semantic calculus.

With Schuon, on the other hand, in an exposition that makes use of a certain "poetic" coloring and flexibility, the author persuades us that he is a witness to truths whose very being he shares. This is not to infer the superiority of one approach over the other, but to accentuate the unique characteristic of Schuon's elucidation of the metaphysics of art, one that is otherwise without precedent in its power to illuminate the spiritual, psychological, and productive significance of art in all its applications. Schuon's observations, one might add, are made all the more radical and, at times, astringent by the nature of the errors they are meant to challenge.

---

[1] A Bibliography of these can be found in Frithjof Schuon, *Art from the Sacred to the Profane: East and West*, edited by Catherine Schuon (Bloomington, IN: World Wisdom, 2007), which is an anthology of selected passages assembled from the writings in question.

⇥⇢✦⇠⇤

As has already been hinted, the reader will quickly go astray here if it is not recognized that, in common with the whole of his writings, the necessary sense of valuation and judgment in his discussion of art is established on the fundamental distinction between the Absolute and the relative—the necessary being of the Supreme Principle that, sufficient unto itself "cannot not be" and which, through its transcendent and immanent modes, reverberates through the relative cosmic substance in order to affirm its unicity in each and every formal expression. This macrocosmic "operation" is recapitulated in the human microcosm in virtue of the totality and objectivity of intelligence.

This totality of intelligence permits man to stand apart, mentally and creatively, from the phenomenal flow that is both his inner and outer experience. Thus he is able to situate himself, according to substantial values, within a hierarchy of knowledge, the order of which is symbolic of the unity of all things in their first principle. This explains a noticeable characteristic of Schuon's exposition in which whatever the point at issue, whatever the theme requiring explication, the explication itself has an eye to all levels of being, so that art is here always placed within the context of a sapiential knowledge rather than accorded a quasi-absolute and therefore idolatrous status of itself. These writings never grant an invalid "absolute" value to contingent modes of thought and judgment.

This being the case one cannot turn to these texts for the sort of analysis and assessment that more commonly passes for the study of art and aesthetics—the elaboration of theories and valuations in which no account is taken of the relativities of human thought and action in the light of the ultimate principle of life. In Schuon's writings we have a series of fundamental observations, not systematically propounded, but assuredly essentially comprehensive, that with the utmost transparency reveal the interrelationship uniting intelligence, spirituality, nature, the senses, creativity, work, skill, and human destiny as they are prefigured in man as he is created in the Divine Image. In virtue of this transparency, Schuon's thesis, adducing some reflection of the Divine in the least act of thinking and making properly performed, sustains a cognitive conviction that transcends the usual categories of art theorists and historians.

In so far as these writings are a recall to the order of mental orthodoxy they are a reminder of the central importance of Beauty as the dynamic principle at the heart of aesthetic experience—for the latter is merely an animal function if it is not transfigured by a contemplative dynamic that moves the soul away from the diversity and dissipation that is worldliness as such.

In so far as these writings are a corrective of orientation of spiritual volition they are a reminder of the symbolic function of nature as a sanctuary that nurtures those resonances of affinity that exist between God's creation and the theomorphic principle of human creation. These writings never for a moment lose sight of the fact that the order and orientation provided by art (traditionally, the principle of manifestation of forms in perfect work) in all its manifold applications and detail has an intimate bearing on every stage of the journey of the human soul towards its destiny. Here, the overarching requirements needed for the realization of that last end are the adjuvant function of art towards "what alone matters as regards our latter end . . . that one should have a qualitative, and symbolically adequate, notion of cosmic causality in as much as it regulates our posthumous destinies".

If humanism amounts to the process whereby the idea that man is created in the Divine Image is gradually eroded, then modernism is the process whereby man's theomorphic nature is finally eradicated. Once this has been achieved, as the last century bears witness, only questions of technique remain—hence the machine; hence the whole industrial milieu; hence man's alienation from nature and the modern world as we know it. This same world is one in which it is willfully forgotten that the works of man can only possess value and meaning on the basis that there are realities of the Spirit beyond the mere construing of matter and that man has realizable affinities with those realities.

Modern art, based as it is on the elevation of spontaneity and innovation as "absolute" value, forgets that man only has need for what is truly useful, a fact that presupposes a certain limit of equilibrium in the production and arrangement of the arts of life. Beyond that the exponential growth of fabricated things, whether as mental theories, works of art, or material products, becomes counter-productive. For this natural law of balance between inner and outer, once breached, becomes disastrous as the body of objective experience becomes subjectively unsupportable. Schuon, by implication, points to the parallel between this development in modern art and its analogous development in the modern material sciences, a development that is irreconcilable "with the ends of human intelligence" and which is for that reason spiritually unsustainable.

Once the theomorphic "pattern" is removed from the human microcosm then the human state as such is reduced exclusively to the capacity of its insufficiencies so that art, instead of taking the measure of what man ought to become, runs the risk (a risk it is seldom, in practice, unable to avoid) of being the measure of his diminishment. Such aberrations of contemporary art as "reflect the human condition" (as they are so frequently characterized) are noticeable for their reductive criteria in which there is no adequate or operative sense of objectivity and subjectivity—hence no acknowledgment that intelligence demands some means of weighing the extent to which truth is in all circumstances imposed upon man in virtue of the very objectivity of his total intelligence.

The *raison d'être* of the human state, as Schuon constantly reminds us, and all the paradoxes that flow from it, can be traced back to the fact of man being created in the image of God. Which is why art that has only a human character (Schuon allows for the "sensible consolations" afforded by such an art "with a view to an equilibrium conducive to the spiritual life, rather in the manner of the flowers and birds in a garden"), can have an air of contrivance and superfluity that traps man in the confines of what he has failed to become. Such art, naturalism, and worse, its perversions, lacks that essential dimension which would lend it both an integral dignity and a formal transparency in the face of a Truth that is always more than man can embody merely by the sum of his thoughts and actions. In the final analysis art must have a spiritual content because the spiritual is man's true vocation.

The relationship between God and man can be understood in this analogous sense: ocular vision proves the existence of a world outside the human subject, but the objectivity of that world cannot be known outside the "subjective" mode of the intelligence. Subject and object must therefore partake of the same cognitive reality. The presence of the intellect in man proves the existence of God as an "other", both beyond and within the interiority of consciousness, for man cannot be at one and the same time both the author and comprehender of cognitive reality. God is both that transcendent and immanent reality to which our being and knowing are called. Just as there is no division of consciousness between the observed and the observer in the act of vision, so there is no essential division of intellect between man and God in the direct intuition of being. Hence Schuon's characterization of intelligence as "total" and "objective".

The importance of artistic form is due to the fact that Beauty is the cognitive agent that, as it were, permeates both cosmic illusion (*māyā*) and human perception (ugliness is always a deviation from the real) in order to demonstrate the latter's sufficient and direct affinity with the Absolute without recourse to reflexive thought, according to the principle that like is known by like. Were this not the case then the beauties of nature would be entirely invalid as symbols of support to intellection—as if God had made the world to be of diverse effects that in no way reflect their causes in an ultimate principle of unity. In which case the forms of nature (*natura naturata*) would be models of total deception, instead of, as is the case, the substratum of an illusion that exhibits the structure or play of cosmic forces. If external manifestation were to have no relation to the truth of an internal essence then all cognitive action would be an arbitrary exercise wedded to invincible error—a process in which pleasure and truth could have no effective correspondence. In which case, why art at all, seeing that it is the purpose of art to in some sense convey the truth of Beauty? "The elements of beauty, be they visual or auditive, static or dynamic, are not only pleasant, they are above all true and their pleasantness comes from their truth; this is the most obvious, and yet the least understood truth of aesthetics"—which explains why "the abolition of beauty . . . means the end of the intelligibility of the world".

Homo faber is nothing if not a creature for whom the act of cognition of necessity seeks the true beyond objects of sensation and whose perceptions seek the being beyond appearances; consequently "The full understanding of beauty demands virtue and is identifiable with it. . . . There is a *distinguo* to make, in sensing the beautiful, between aesthetic sensation and the corresponding beauty of soul."

    beauty → contemplation → recollection
    beauty → aesthesis   → dissipation

Beauty and cognition are fused (but not confused) in an intimacy that is one with our human vocation for "in beauty man 'realizes', passively in his perceptions and externally in his productions of it, that which he himself should 'be' after an active or inward fashion".

⊷⊶◉→❂←◉⊷⊶

Schuon points to the paradox of art: that man, who is after all a part of the creation, must assume the role of creator. Thus, in a sense, he must act as if he were God but in the knowledge that he cannot operate as *homo faber* outside the order of contingent things. Or at least he cannot do so without invoking the suprahuman principle that is within him and by the measure of which he is granted the gift of creation by way of compensation for his fallen condition. Apart from invoking his innermost substance his only other choice, in so far as he may appeal to what is, in a sense, "beyond" him, is to invoke the infra-human—the sub-human—precisely that which plunges him into the insufficiency of the human state as such. There is no other choice.

A related paradox: *homo faber* cannot, like God, create from *nothing*. The fact that he must create from that which is already created means that strictly speaking he re-creates. To "create" from what is already created brings him up against the defining limits of subjectivity and objectivity—inner and outer worlds. Is the substance of art to be merely a solipsist agenda or an untransfigured naturalism? In the former case how can any artist, as subject, be more worthy of consideration than any other subject? In the latter case how can any artist's perceptions and their expressive manifestation be more "valid" than those of any other artist, seeing that the absolute objectivity of human perception, though it can be embodied, cannot be proven? The more the modernist agenda of art closes upon the *reductio ad absurdum* of its own activity, so it comes to embody the extremes of this relativist dilemma, to the point where it becomes impossible to distinguish art from non-art.

In either case—that of solipsism and that of naturalism—a limit is imposed upon works of art such as to undermine any justification for their being called into existence for the sake of a human good. The ultimate justification of such a good is that it opens on to a plenitude that goes beyond, in the case of a solipsist art, the arbitrary projections of subjectivity, and in the case of naturalism, the veil of externality that clothes appearances. For what other purpose would man want an art other than to take him beyond the limited disclosures of his own subjectivity on the one hand and external appearances on the other?

The specifically human task of the artist is to be a legitimate translator of works, first mentally conceived and then realized outwardly according to the spiritual content of his intelligence and not according to the passional energies of his soul. If art is essential it is because it is the vehicle of beauty and beauty—as Schuon time and again insists—is identified with Being and virtue. If modern man is content to consider Beauty as an optional attribute of sensation, while regarding the practical as a necessity of the material order, that is because he builds a division within himself—he divides the spiritual from the material, the essential from the inessential among the means to life because he will not be persuaded of the law by which no means can ever serve an end that is not already presupposed in those means—the spiritual *in* the material.

A legitimate art is one that recognizes that the world is beauty and that all human actions, making and doing, from the most humble task discharged with right mindfulness, to the building of cathedrals, must in some measure return us to the beauty from whence we have come.

The Absolute in its immanent and transcendent modes in relation to normal art: the crafts attempt to seize upon the immanent essence of substance; the major arts (i.e. architecture) seek to embody the conception of a transcendent principle. The one penetrates to the "secret" of what comes commonly to hand; the other soars to the height of what has been revealed. No purpose is served by insisting that these are exclusive categories.

William Blake: Art as Divine Vision

In ways that are far from obvious, the current popularity of Blake rests, indirectly, upon the large body of Blake scholarship that has grown up around his works since the 1950s. This has more than made up for his being neglected in his lifetime. Even if this scholarly attention has not made the interpretation of his work entirely straightforward, it has certainly dispensed with the notion that Blake was, in his own peculiar way, an untutored naif. There is general agreement among scholars that Blake had access to a considerable body of religious, philosophic, and cultural knowledge, from Plato to his own time. Much of this knowledge was certainly unfashionable in Blake's day. Some of it has come to seem, in our time, to lie at the root of many of the concerns that beset the modern world.

In particular, Blake's castigation of the rationalist, empirical mentality of the so-called Enlightenment thought that was the legacy of his age is now something of a rallying call for those who would challenge the hegemony of the secular materialism of our own day. Blake's inspired, visionary thinking, for many of us, now seems to point to the active assimilation of spiritual realities whose absence has built a world in its own image: a world in which it seems increasingly likely the human race cannot survive.

Yet for much of this scholarship Blake's call to spiritual awakening is not heard. This we must challenge—even if, in the final analysis, we must concede that it is likely that Blake's work will always benefit from painstaking unraveling by informed scholarship. Such unraveling is made necessary by the cross-currents of influence at work from within the patterned compound of his many sources: from myth, politics, history, mysticism, religion, hermeticism, not to mention his own visionary iconography.

To be precise, what must be challenged is the idea that only such scholarship, in so far as it aims to lay bare the meaning of Blake's work in the ebb and flow of borrowed ideas, images, and the history of his own time, can adequately represent this singular artist's full intention. Whatever causal connections may be brought to light along these lines we must nevertheless acknowledge if we are to remain faithful to the overwhelming sense of momentum behind his work, that Blake constantly invites us to rise above our psycho-physical existence to the level that befits us as spiritual beings. The urgency of his polemic all but *defies* us not to feel the impress of his exaltation, his conviction that we must trace our true nature to the elevated level of its divine origin: "The Man who never in his Mind & Thoughts travel'd to Heaven Is No Artist" (458),[1] as he wrote in the margin of Reynolds' *Discourses*. The purpose of this journey to Heaven was "To open the immortal Eyes of Man inwards . . . into Eternity ever expanding in the Bosom of God, the Human Imagination" (623). It was in such terms that Blake conceived of all men, at least potentially, as being artists. Blake composed no special work that outlines his philosophy of art. His *Descriptive Catalogue* is the nearest he came to a formal treatise, containing "Mr. B.'s Opinions and Determinations on Art, very necessary to be known" (562). But his *Vision of the Last Judgment* and the *Annotations to Reynolds* tell us far more about these "Determinations".

If there can be said to be a single statement that concentrates the essence of Blake's philosophy of art it must surely be, "One Power alone makes a Poet: Imagination, The Divine Vision" (782). This is Blake challenging Wordsworth's inventory of the powers needed for the production of poetry: observation, description, and sensibility. We note here, as always with Blake, his insistence on the active presence of the vertical dimension of the Spirit, as opposed to the passive, reflective, horizontal continuities that comprise the temporal dimension. For Blake there is no art that is not in some sense spiritual knowledge, "Prayer is the Study of Art" (776). Blake's "Divine Vision" is nothing less than the irreducible act of cognition, the intuitive moment of the intelligence that descends from beyond the temporal process that is the passage of time flowing from future into past. It is the moment *out* of time that discloses the eternal core of the Real.

---

[1] References in parentheses are to page numbers of Blake, *Complete Writings*, edited by Geoffrey Keynes (Oxford: Oxford University Press, 1966).

It may well be that works of art are aided in their birth by the linear, reflective continuities of memory, observation, material substance, and operative habit that are necessary to the embodiment of any artistic idea. But such continuities do not account for the origin of the idea; that which is outside the process of embodiment and calls it into being in the first place.

> For in this Period the Poet's Work is Done, and all the Great
> Events of Time start forth & are conceiv'd in such a Period,
> Within a Moment, a Pulsation of the Artery. (516)

This is the inscrutable act of cognition that, in its instantaneity, cannot be reduced to the mental and empirical forces that inevitably influence the shaping of a work of art. When Blake asks, "shall Painting be confined to the sordid drudgery of facsimile representations of merely mortal and perishing substances" (576), he is defending the ultimate agency, the supra-temporal intellect that is the true cause of a work of art's coming into being. Whenever the claim is made that we do not know *where* ideas come from, we are acknowledging the fact that the human intellect is a reflection, on the plane of individual consciousness, of the Divine Intellect that can never be reduced to the mechanism of our thought processes. Similarly, the cause of the "idea" of a true work of art can never be equated with the mind/body causality on which it depends for its realization. This is the substance of Blake's affirmation that "Generation" should be "swallow'd up in Regeneration" (533). For him, the eternal, inscrutable "gateway" to the Divine Intellect is the locus of Imagination. It is the *place* where the mundane realities of the temporal world are "Regenerated" in the intellect, finding there the iconography of their eternal reality. For Blake the alliance of art with spirituality is precisely the necessity to live in "Imagination". The condition of our being, the Divine within us, is Imagination: "Man is All Imagination. God is Man & exists in us & we in him" (775).

Blake's advocacy of the supremacy of "Divine Vision" explains his reluctance to develop a systematic theory of art. This would be to reduce, in Reynold's words, "the idea of beauty to general principles" (461)—an idea which Blake castigates. This rejection goes hand in hand with his rejection of the discursive, reasoning faculty (what he called the "Specter"), as the sole arbiter of knowledge, that formed the basis of the Enlightenment philosophies of mind: "Reason, or A Ratio of All we have Known, is not the Same it shall be when we know More" (475).

These last words—"when we know More"—echo, as is often the case with Blake, a formulation of traditional wisdom. In this case, it is the doctrine that whatever is known is known *not* according to the power of the thing that is known, but according to the capacity of the knower. We will see shortly how this enlargement of the frame of reference of the knower alters the perception of the "Ratio of All".

The approach to knowledge was for Blake an act of intuitive apprehension, an uncovering of the "Eye of Imagination", so as to see the "Permanent Realities of Every Thing we see reflected in this Vegetable Glass of Nature" (605). What is ultimately Real, "while it is altogether hidden from Corporeal Understanding", addresses itself "to the Intellectual powers" (825). That is, unpremeditated intuition; "Knowledge is not by deduction, but Immediate by Perception or Sense at once. Christ addresses [note the present tense referring, not to the historical Christ, but to the ever-living incarnation of the Divine Presence] himself to the Man, not to his Reason" (774). Blake's "Determinations" on the nature of art and man, and especially his concept of Imagination, are alike statements about what is Real at the heart of human experience. A philosophy of aesthetics as the rationalization of our "animal attachment to sensation" (to borrow a phrase from A. K. Coomaraswamy), was anathema to Blake: "The Natural Body is an Obstruction to the Soul or Spiritual Body" (775). In opposition to the philosophy of art as having to do with the expression of purely psycho-physical reactions—the fabrications of the "daughters of Memory"—he posited the visions of the "daughters of Inspiration": that is "Imagination . . . a Representation of what Eternally Exists, Really & Unchangeably" (604). Thus, art is the need to incarnate "The Eternal Body of Man . . . The Imagination, that is God himself. The Divine Body, Jesus: we are his Members. It manifests itself in his Works of Art" (776).

We can see from this last statement that Blake's central doctrine, though idiosyncratic in the way it identifies Jesus with Imagination, none the less rests upon the traditional analogy of the human artist as working in the manner of operation of the Divine Artificer—the Creator.

Since for Blake Imagination *is* Jesus, and Jesus is the Incarnation of the Logos, then Imagination is the manifestation of the Divine "making" as an act of Being. Thus, the human making of a work of art through the inspiration of Imagination, is by analogy an act of making manifest the eternal forms of things as they are inherent as possibilities of the Divine Intellect. For Blake, "Imagination" is the Divine Intellect reflected in the individual mind. It is the true image bearing light that illuminates the mind with the ideal forms inherent in Being. "The form of a thing", wrote Boethius, "is like a light by which that thing is known". In essence, Blake agrees: "All Things are comprehended in their Eternal Forms in the divine body of the Savior, the True Vine of Eternity, the Human Imagination" (605-606). These forms are consubstantial with the Light that is the Divine form of Being itself—"The light that lighteth every man that cometh into the world", in the words of the Gospel. Which explains why, in Blake's words, "The human mind cannot go beyond the gifts of God, the Holy Ghost" (579).

These forms, however, are not vague, remote abstractions in comparison with the perceptions of empirical observation. They "are not, as the modern philosophy supposes, a cloudy vapor, or a nothing: they are organized and minutely articulated beyond all the mortal and perishing nature can produce" (576). Such forms articulate precisely, because each of them is, as it were, the individual, pre-phenomenal "name" of the qualitative essence of each thing as it is inherent in the eternal act of creation. Blake refers to these "names" when he states that, "All deities reside in the human breast" (153) in virtue of the fact that "Human Nature is the image of God" (83). He also clearly states: "These Gods are visions of the eternal attributes, or divine names" (571). Thus, in aiding the apprehension of the "Divine Body" they "ought to be the servants and not the masters of man or of society" (571), for they are the witness to the innermost certainty of the cognitive act. When "erected into [idols they] become destructive to humanity" (571).

Whereas empirical vision, always itself changing, can only imprecisely witness the ever-changing phenomenal order of nature, the "divine names" by contrast could not have greater clarity in presenting the absolute reality of what it is that cognition grasps, for they are identical with it. The direct clarity of these "names" must therefore become the artist's iconography. Hence Blake's claim, in his *Descriptive Catalogue*: "The great and golden rule of art, as well as of life, is this: That the more distinct, sharp, and wiry the bounding line, the more perfect the work of art. . . . The want of this determinate and bounding form evidences the want of idea in the artist's mind. . . . Leave out this line, and you leave out life itself; all is chaos again" (585). This "chaos" is nothing less than the data of provisional sensory experience (the "spectrous shadow") devoid of the permanent, intelligible form it needs to make it a true object of knowledge, its "supreme eternal state" (571).

Blake worked with "Clear colors unmuddied by oil, and firm and determinate lineaments unbroken by shadows", so as "to display and not hide form" (564). He hated "that infernal machine called Chiaro Oscuro" (582), knowing that once the artist knew only how to represent, as it were, by rote, the effects of natural light and shade, perspective, and the like, as they appear to the *passive* "perishing, mortal organ of perception", this would weaken the artist's disciplined habit of conceiving the work *actively* in the eye of the imaginative intellect. The Venetian device of treating the effects of light and shade puts "the original Artist in fear and doubt of his own original conception" (582). For Blake, light does not shine *down* on to the objects of sensory perception so much as from within, *out* of Being itself. "Blotting and blurring" shadows could have no place in his expression of the eternal forms of the Divine. His intention was to give shape to the intelligible, not to record sensation.

In the contemplative act of visualization—what Blake refers to as "traveling to Heaven"—the artist grasps the inner, spiritual image which he must imitate in some outward image. In this operation, in the words of St. Thomas, "the form of the intellect is the principle of that operation". For such a task, Blake says, "He who does not imagine in stronger and better lineaments, and in stronger and better light than his perishing and mortal eye can see, does not imagine at all" (576). Only at the intuitive core of the cognitive act of visualization can the truth of the inspired image be grasped, by virtue of the identity of the organ of perception with the primary truth that is its object. This identity lends the act an infallibility. Hence, Blake, in effect agreeing with St. Thomas, says, "Art is Definite & Determinate . . . but by Inspiration & Vision, because Vision is Determinate & Perfect" (457).

This act of intuitive visualization is the highest faculty of imaginative perception, and goes far beyond the "ratio of all we have already known", that is, the natural purview of the "Reasoning Specter" (as Blake calls it): the rational, discriminate faculty of reflexive thought that forms, assesses, and judges the images of mental activity generated by the empirical self's interaction with the world of objects. Blake never uses the word "perhaps". He always speaks with a tone of certainty—like a man who has witnessed the Truth and is thereafter absolutely convinced of what he has seen. He is certain of the superiority of imaginative apprehension over reflective, discriminative perception. He is certain because whereas the latter must always separate the knower from the object of knowledge, imaginative apprehension takes place at the "point" of identity between the act of contemplation and its object. To experience his identity is to enlarge the perception of Reality itself, which is otherwise bounded by empirical limits. It is an irruption of the spiritual into the natural. It breaks the "ratio", the material husk, so to say, to reveal its qualitative essence: "the ratio of all we have already known, is not the same that it shall be when we know more" (97).

Imagination is the source of all truly creative activity because it is identified with the very ground of individual consciousness, being the subject of all cognitive verification: "The Imagination is not a State: It is the Human Existence itself" (522). It is not a state in so far as it is anterior to the directional impulses or modes of the soul:

> Affection or Love becomes a State when divided from Imagination.
> The memory is a State always, & the Reason is a State. . . .
> (522)

The transient states of the soul—reflective thought, memory, sentiment and so on—are activations or determinations of the

"Eternal Human". Whereas, cumulatively, these modes of the soul amount to consciousness of the individual human existence, they do not constitute or establish the sufficient principle of Universal Being "in which the Spirit travels" (680). The reality of the states is provisional from the perspective of the "Eternal Human". But from the perspective of their determinations, "The Spiritual States of the Soul are all Eternal" (681). Man may pass on "but States remain for Ever" (606). The need to pass on is energized by man's innate need to embrace the fullness of Being that is his proper nature, for "The bounded is loathed by its possessor. The same dull round, even of a universe, would soon become a mill with complicated wheels" (97). Thus "The desire of Man being Infinite, the possession is Infinite & himself Infinite" (97).

In the true fullness of the "Eternal Human", man moves beyond the level of consciousness in which the contents of mental activity are known according to the relationships of distinctness and difference. The "new Ratio" is created when the content of mental activity is known in the permanence of its dwelling in the Divine nature of the Infinite. What if it were not possible to go beyond the finite? "If it were not for the Poetic or Prophetic character the Philosophic & Experimental would soon be at the ratio of all things, & stand still, unable to do other than repeat the same dull round over again" (97). The implication is clear: this would be spiritual torment.

Because, for Blake, art is the instrumental means of Imagination, and Imagination is the instrumental means of the Divine Principle within, the exercise of art is to bring about the coincidence of being and knowing. This means that it is not possible to separate his doctrine of art from his doctrine of man. One of the most important doctrines spanning the breadth of his thought on art and man is the notion that the Infinite is found in and *through* the finite: "He who sees the Infinite in all things, sees God. He who sees the Ratio only, sees himself only" (98). The Infinite is the qualitative core that abides at the very root of finite things. It is the infallible signature that guarantees that the forms of the Creation are a revelation of the Divine Body. Otherwise they would be "outside" of God; something that is contrary to the manifestation of the totality of possibilities that is the nature of the Divine Principle. These finite forms are "Every Thing we see reflected in this Vegetable Glass of Nature" (605). They are perceived by man's natural faculties of sense, thereby veiling the Infinite. The purpose of art is to lift the veil that is this "Generated Body": in the famous words of the opening of "Auguries of Innocence", it is

> To see a World in a Grain of Sand
> And a Heaven in a Wild Flower.
> Hold Infinity in the Palm of your hand
> And Eternity in an hour. (431)

This idea of Blake's rests upon the primary analogy of the law of cosmic correspondence: that this world is a "shadow" or copy of the unmanifest world of Eternal Reality. That is to say, what is "above" is mirrored in what is "below"; with the added corollary that, in Blake's words, "What is Above is Within, for every-thing in Eternity is translucent".

> tho it appears Without, it is Within,
> In your Imagination, of which this world of Mortality is but a
>   Shadow. (709)

Blake is here simply echoing traditional doctrine in seeing the natural world as being patterned on a supra-natural model—the original of the earthly model being laid up in Heaven. There is no dualism involved in this. But there is duality. It must be understood that Heaven and earth denote in the mode of polarity, the primary determination towards the generation of multiplicity from the Unity of the Divine Oneness. Everything in Heaven and earth is a significant part of the Divine economy. Everything has its meaning and value from being generated from the One. For this reason, Blake asserts: "Poetry admits not a Letter that is Insignificant, so Painting admits not a Grain of Sand or a Blade of Grass Insignificant" (611). But, at times, he could exaggerate. Out of his certainty he could claim that he failed to recognize the finite, natural world at all! "I assert for My Self that I do not behold the outward Creation" (617). But Blake never hints that the world is less than it ought to be. Indeed, we get from his art a vivid sense that all that takes place in the world of Heaven and earth has the dynamic of cosmic necessity. For it to be otherwise would point to some insufficiency on the part of the Creator. This explains why Blake does not idolize nature. Nor does he idealize it. His imaginative vision transcends the deficiencies of natural perception on the one hand, and the abstractions of purely mental images on the other. In viewing the phenomenal forms of external Nature *through* the eye and not *with* the eye, he finds the Infinite embodied within, articulated in nature's "minute particulars".

If, in Blake's cosmology, infinite and finite, eternal and temporal worlds interpenetrate, none the less a tension is set up between them, owing to the dual nature of man. For Blake, as for Genesis, "Human nature is the image of God". The person of Christ offers proof of this since he would not have been manifested in human form were that form unfit to receive and express the Divine nature. Thus, as a reflection of the Divine Intellect man has his being on the plane of intelligence, while on the existential plane, he is a direct image or projection of God the Divine Artist (through whom all things are made), since man alone on earth can formally choose to create works of art. Yet, owing to the Fall, man is created in the duality of a "Natural" and a "Spiritual Body". And since, as we have already noted, Blake holds that "The Natural Body is an Obstruction to the Soul or Spiritual Body" (775), so the natural man (Blake's "Selfhood"), is continuously "at Enmity with God" (782). This enmity is the occasion in man for the struggle he must undergo to attach himself to what is permanently Real. The whole emphasis of Blake's doctrine of man—with obvious repercussions for his doctrine of art—is summed up in the urgency of these lines from *Milton*:

> Judge then of thy Own Self: thy Eternal Lineaments explore,
> What is Eternal & what Changeable, & what Annihilable.
> (522)

The relationship of beauty to art is clearly stated by Blake: "The Beauty proper for sublime art is lineaments, or forms and features that are capable of being the receptacles of intellect" (579–80). Here again, Blake opposes the Enlightenment mentality for which beauty belongs to the order of natural perception. "Knowledge of Ideal Beauty", says Blake, challenging Reynolds, "is

Not to be acquired. It is Born with us. Innate Ideas are in Every Man . . . they are truly Himself" (459).

Beauty is latent in intellect by reason of the fact that, in the words of St. Thomas' formulation of the doctrine, "The Being of all things derives from the Divine Beauty". We have already noted that, for Blake, to receive no more than "the Vegetable Glass of nature by man's mortal perishing organs", is to descend into the chaos of the unintelligible. Thus, if Beauty has its formal cause in knowledge, then the beauty of art must be incompatible with that which is without intelligible form. For this reason, any vague or chance element in a work of art must be deemed a defect. Such defects must indicate a deprivation of the "light" of intellect. They manifest a measure of indeterminacy ("All Sublimity is founded on Minute Discrimination" [453]) in the artist's conception of his work in Imagination—his "Eternal Body". In the event, what is expressed by a failed work of art, which in Blake's terms would be one dependent upon memory of external realities, is not the "particular" truth of some intended referent, but a recollection of sense perception that is not born of the Intellect, the "Bosom of God" (123). It is to see the "Ratio" rather than the "Infinite". Blake outlines the process in his *Vision of the Last Judgment*:

> General Knowledge is Remote Knowledge; It is in Particulars that Wisdom consists & Happiness too. Both in Art & in Life, General Masses are as Much Art as a Pasteboard Man is Human. . . . He who enters into & discriminates most minutely the Manners & Intentions [and] Characters in all their branches, is the alone Wise or Sensible Man & on this discrimination All Art is founded . . . not a line is drawn without intention, & that most discriminate and particular. (611)

The presiding characteristic of Blake's thought, implicit in the above passage, is an emphasis on the ever-present need for spiritual vigilance and the consequent·reckoning of failing to perfect one's art:

> Some people flatter themselves that there will be No Last Judgment & that Bad Art will be adopted & mixed with Good Art, That Error or Experiment will make a part of Truth. . . .

These people flatter themselves. . . . Error is Created. Truth is
Eternal. . . . Error . . . will be Burned up. (617)

In this "testing" of human works by fire Blake is perhaps echoing
I Corinthians 3:13-14.

Because in terms of Blake's cosmology knowledge is Being,
artistic "sin" must be seen as the failure to realize our true nature,
in the way that darkness is an absence of light. The Last Judgment,
pronounced against "Bad Art", is therefore Judgment against the
self—the ignorance of the "Generated Body": "What are the Pains
of Hell but Ignorance, Bodily Lust, Idleness & devastation of the
things of the Spirit?" (717).

The Judgment that is the ignorance of the "Generated Body"
cannot, by definition, come from the "Generated Body" itself.
From what vantage point could such a judgment gain its purchase?
The interpretation that suggests itself here, one fully in keeping
with Blake's doctrine of man, is this: by virtue of the deiformity
of the human substance—"Human Nature is the image of God"
(83)—the fullest life of man is a total realization of his spiritual
potential. To turn away from this potential in order to concentrate
on the sensory consolations of the natural body, is to prefer the
things of this world to the things of God. So, at the point of death,
the divine potential as such has oversight of what the individual
has accomplished, for good or ill, and judges accordingly.

The "sin" of the natural man (in Blake's terms, the "non-
artist") is to be cast into "a world of Generation & death" (613).
This he must cast off: "No man can Embrace True Art till he has
Explor'd & cast out False Art" (613). In doing so he is enabled
to converse "with Eternal Realities as they Exist in the Human
Imagination" (613). These are innate since "Man is Born Like a
Garden ready Planted & Sown" (471). The "Eternal Realities"
are latent in the "Divine Imagination", which itself lends being
to all things. When the artist, through his original conception, or
the spectator, through the work of art, enters into one of these
"Realities", he or she experiences an intuition of archetypal or
Ideal Beauty: "Art can never exist without Naked Beauty dis-
played" (776). This experience is akin to the highest level of con-
scious being. It is impossible to analyze, being known directly and
at once in the modes of intellect and ecstasy. In this experience is

the very signature of our being. As Blake explains in another passage from the *Vision of the Last Judgment*:

> If the Spectator could Enter into these Images in his Imagination, approaching them on the Fiery Chariot of his Contemplative Thought, if he could Enter into Noah's Rainbow or into his bosom, or could make a Friend & Companion of one of these Images of wonder, which always entreats him to leave mortal things (as he must know), then would he arise from his Grave, then would he meet the Lord in the Air & then he would be happy. (611)

Here we have the heart of Blake's vision of the proper vocation of man. Since no man can be without activities that have consequences, "The Whole Business of Man Is The Arts and All Things Common. . . . The unproductive Man is not a Christian" (777). The practice of any productive activity becomes a hindrance to spiritual growth only when it is "Manual Labor", that is "a work of no Mind" (598). Such mechanical servitude stifles the possibility that the outward work may contribute to the corresponding inner realization engendered by "Persisting in Spiritual Labors & the Use of that Talent which it is Death to Bury, & of that Spirit to which we are called" (863). The outcome of the work of mechanical servitude, can only be "destructive of Humanity & of Art" (603), and by extension, its products satisfy only the appetites and desires of the spectral "Selfhood" of the "Natural Man". When, in society at large, it becomes the dominant means of the productive economy, "Art Degraded, Imagination Denied, War Governed the Nations" (775).

By contrast, the exercise of our inborn "Talent" leads to the restitution of "The Primeval State of Man [that is] Wisdom, Art, and Science" (621). The artificer who molds himself after the Divine pattern works in the light of the principle that God's will must "be done on earth as it is in Heaven". Only then, Blake insists, will "The Lord our father . . . do for us & with us according to his Divine will for our Good" (802).

We could not see more clearly than in this last thought Blake's call to spiritual awakening. And in the foregoing we have seen Blake's unequivocal statement of the terms by which, in his view, such an awakening might take place. His idiosyncratic identity of Jesus with "Imagination", God within; his insistence on the direct perception of archetypal realities by Imagination, the "Eternal Body of Man"; the "Divine Body" in man, over and above the obstruction of the "Natural Body" on the one hand and the "Vegetable Glass of Nature" on the other. This is no purely subjective process. It is not even a state of the soul. It is the "Eternal Human" itself by which man, as artist, participates directly in the "Divine Reality".

It must strike us that Blake's terms are very far from the concerns that generally engage an artist in our time, a time in which his work has a wider circulation than ever before. No doubt this paradox is at least partially explained by the fact that both his literary and his visual works speak powerfully of a level of vision that is all but absent from contemporary forms of artistic expression. Blake's "Vision" addresses a subject for which modern man, alienated as he is from the perception and acknowledgment of spiritual realities, nonetheless, feels a deep nostalgia. In an age that is wary of the availability of absolutes, that is tired of the inanities of solipsism, and skeptical of the affirmation of certainties, Blake offers a unique challenge. His works present the possibility that the primary concerns of the human condition, derided and obscured as they have become, especially in the field of the arts, may yet be offered to our contemplation as a viable alternative to the prevailing, reductionist humanism (and worse) that currently debilitates their practice.

AFTERWORD

As was suggested at the outset, each of the foregoing studies, sometimes directly sometimes by implication, recognizes the need to bring together two opposing worlds: the sacred and the secular, the traditional and the modern, the human and, perhaps, the post-human. By further implication and cumulatively the obvious question arises: "the times are out of joint, what is to be done?" The answer, according to the nature of the case, is complex and must take account of many deeply-seated factors. Some of these are far from obvious and some our age is reluctant to admit.

Work is part of the active life, the domain of causes and effects, where the application of productive effort (cause) has some outward result (effect). The value given to any such operation will depend entirely upon the way we conceive of their agent. If to be human is to be little more than a body of energies and appetites then the means adopted to satisfy those appetites will bear little scrutiny beyond seeing that our desires are met as expeditiously as possible. If, on the other hand, to be human is to be created in God's image, the situation has more far-reaching consequences. In a world of traditional values, and in respect of any human activity, the question of what is conducive to man's theomorphic nature was the primary and underlying orientation: at prayer, at play and, in some respects most importantly, at work. To this end the traditional order of values that prevailed in the day-to-day world until, more or less, the seventeenth century, had as its purpose to refer all being, thinking, and doing back ("upwards") to the first ("highest") cause. This is where, according to the traditional vision of the nature of man in the Creation, the permanent and sustaining reality of things was located—*is* a presence at once transformative and abiding over and against the impermanence and flux of the created order.

The modalities of practical application that make up the world of work functioned in the traditional order with a view to allowing man *in* his work to come to some realization of the inner, supra-human basis of his existence. In recognition of this was, for instance, Eric Gill's insistence that he was not concerned with what the worker got *from* work, but with what he got *by* working. In this traditional view work is as much a contemplative as a practical activity. Of necessity and expediently this no doubt restrained the natural expansion of whatever human productivity might be inclined to undertake. It is inevitable that the modern mind, conceiving the human in terms of biological process, would see this as a curtailment of human talent and ability. A global economy that is fuelled by unbridled innovation and production has within it nothing integral to act as a restraining impulse to what becomes in the end a process that is destructive of humanity. The fact that the planet now shows signs of protest over our unrelenting onslaught upon its "resources" may well give pause for thought. But it is not as part of the economic process itself that the question of restraint arises. We have grown used to a system of manufacture that provides goods that were beyond the dreams (as certainly the needs) of our ancestors. And this by means of products in which, to all intents and purposes, the specifically human cannot be present. Precisely, our "needs" have been multiplied exponentially as the motive energy of the system itself. Of those needs the spiritual benefits that inhere in workmanship—such as countless generations have borne witness—the system eradicates.

All this must be taken into account whenever any attempt is made to address the question "what is to be done?" For the question cannot even be framed without implying that there must be present in the mind some vision of what man is and what might be his appropriate end. This last is the ultimate question so far as man's existential life is concerned, and no answer to an ultimate question can be forthcoming from within the sphere of human activity itself. Action leads to further action as a response; it cannot turn in upon itself to seek the rightful or wrongful direction of its impulses. Before doing there is being—which is to say knowledge, which is to say wisdom. Wisdom is not the province of action, else we would not have the world we have.

The transposition from the human to the Divine that is envisaged in the traditional order of values is made via the bridge that was the science of symbols—nothing less than a wisdom about the transparency of the phenomenal order that demands that there be a harmony and a reciprocity as between archetypal principles and their embodiment in being and doing, thought and action. We can hardly pretend that what amounts to an accord between Heaven and earth is the operative, spiritual norm—the "bridge"—in our post-industrial world. In point of fact, this latter world exists only in so far as it acts as a repudiation of the traditional wisdom and order.

Each of the subjects presented here has, in their own way and according to their gifts, made a distinctive contribution to the affirmation of that "bridge", the necessity of which was remarked at the outset. With Edward Johnston and Eric Gill we have, as it were, a complementary pair. The starting point of Gill's polemic was the question "What is Man?" From this central question his answers move outwards, like the spokes of a wheel, to touch upon the implications of man's theomorphic nature in so far as it has a consequence in the fields of religion, beauty, art, morality, and aesthetics as well as more widely; what the question's application might contribute to the living fabric of a holy tradition of working. Not that the focus of his attention was in any way vague or too generalized. It was, after all, based on an intimate and detailed experience—not to say mastery—of several fields of craftsmanship. As a religious apologist he is still undervalued. Peter Faulkner has recorded how D. H. Lawrence read Gill's *Art Nonsense* on his deathbed and thought it contained more wisdom than "all Karl Marx or Whitehead or a dozen other philosophers rolled together".

With his close friend Johnston it is otherwise. The dispositive impulse that led Gill outward in Johnston moved inwards, concentrating on matters in hand, literally. It is as if the calligrapher was concerned to sense and interpret the sacramental inherence of the hand; in the pressure of the scribe's instrument upon the writing surface. Here there is an immediacy, a tactile intimacy of experience that springs directly from an acute sensitivity to the noumenal presence in the work of the hand.

W. R. Lethaby was himself a bridge between the pioneering generation of William Morris and the modern industrial world. His was a courageous attempt to formulate and defend a set of practical rules whereby handiwork might have a valid application in a world of rapidly mechanizing production. But even more than for the record of his work he is to be valued as a generous and wise teacher and inspirer of others. Certainly Gill thought so.

It fell to Coomaraswamy to chart the metaphysical, cosmological, and cultural foundations that form the principled underpinnings of art and work that Lethaby's thought could not provide. And this Coomaraswamy demonstrated by means of a rigorous and unparalleled scholarship that showed the universality of their application. Here at last was a comprehensive, intellectually and spiritually sound body of wisdom as to what constitutes an authentic sacramental bond between God and work.

If there is a single word that might characterize the multiple talents of William Blake it must surely be "transformation". Blake earned a meager living as a jobbing engraver. The sprawling energies of his creative genius, however, found expression in his poetry and painting. These have, in essence, a single message. Here was a man who was never, in anything he did, out of contact with the noumenal order of reality, which he experienced as the true source of that "vegetable kingdom" that is the existential envelope of man's daily existence. With Blake all worldly, sensory, remembered experience remains unreal until it is transformed by the Divine power of its inherent nature. With Blake it is as if God and work were one and the same informing energy.

In his deceptively simple formulation—"art is the perfection of work"—Frithjof Schuon encapsulates the universal and proper kinship of art to workmanship. Schuon's statements on art form a relatively small part of the whole of his writings, which last provide their integral context. This amounts to a profound understanding of the role of beauty—from its cosmological dimension to its personal and affective properties—in relation to sapiential experience. These singular chapters bring home to us an authentic vision of the contemplative basis of all human being and doing, whether it has as its end some practical result of a more overtly spiritual goal. In a series of extraordinarily nuanced insights Schuon leaves us in no doubt as to the impossibility of their being, ultimately, disjunct worlds of sacred and secular, spiritual and existential experience: except, it must be said, in so far as a downward precipitation of the ego is allowed to exert itself. Schuon never underestimates, never dilutes with misplaced optimism, never clouds with sentimentality, or finds intractable to heavy-handed fatalism, the dire consequences of this down-ward pressure that marks the "latter days" it is our destiny to live through. The nuancing of his presentation is a powerful and timely reminder of the inward and essential dimension that must be granted its proper place and effectiveness in any attempt to re-unite the productive impulse with its roots in spiritual experience. This essential dimension, principally beauty of soul in relation to the metaphysical transparency of phenomenal reality, through symbolism, alone secures Primordial Beauty as the norm of all cognition, perception, and action.

The subjects we have considered, collectively, bear testimony to the inclusiveness that must inform any remedial action under-taken to heal our wounds. There can be no remedy for that soul-anaesthetizing agitation that all too often accompanies work in the post-industrial world. If the work of God is seen to have no place in the work of man, then we cannot expect our working efforts to be redeemed by any consequence that proceeds from merely human endeavor. A godless world is by default and definition a human world—precisely what stands in need of redemption.

SELECTED BIBLIOGRAPHY

Berry, Wendell. *Standing By Words.* San Francisco, 1983.

———. *Home Economics.* San Francisco, 1987.

———. *The Art of the Commonplace: The Agrarian Essays.* Washington, DC, 2002.

———. "Christianity and the Survival of Creation". In *Sex, Economy, Freedom and Community*, 93-116. New York, 1993. Reprinted in *Seeing God Everywhere: Essays on Nature and the Sacred.* Edited by Barry McDonald. Bloomington, IN, 2003.

Burckhardt, Titus. *Sacred Art in East and West: Its Principles and Methods.* Translated by Lord Northbourne. London, 1967.

———. *Mirror of the Intellect.* Translated by William Stoddart. Cambridge, UK, 1987.

———. *The Foundations of Christian Art: Illustrated.* Edited by Michael Oren Fitzgerald. Bloomington, IN, 2006.

Coomaraswamy, Ananda K. *The Transformation of Nature in Art.* Cambridge, Mass., 1934.

———. *Why Exhibit Works of Art?* London, 1943.

———. *What is Civilisation? and Other Essays.* Ipswich, UK, 1989.

———. *Figures of Speech or Figures of Thought? The Traditional View of Art.* Edited by William Wroth. Bloomington, IN, 2007.

Coomaraswamy, Ananda K., John Howard Benson, and A. Graham Carey. *What Use is Art Anyway?* Newport, 1937.

Coomaraswamy, Ananda K. and A. Graham Carey. *Patron and Artist: Pre-Renaissance and Modern.* Norton, Mass., 1936.

Ellul, Jacques. *The Technological Bluff.* Translated by G. W. Bromiley. Grand Rapids, 1990.

Faulkner, Peter. *William Morris and Eric Gill.* London, 1975.

Gill, Eric. *Art Nonsense and Other Essays.* London, 1929.

————. *Beauty Looks After Herself.* London, 1933.

————. *Work and Leisure.* London, 1935.

————. *It All Goes Together: Selected Essays.* New York, 1944.

————. *A Holy Tradition of Working.* Edited by Brian Keeble. Ipswich, 1983.

Gimpel, Jean. *Against Art and Artists.* Edinburgh, 1991.

Gleizes, Albert. *Life and Death of the Christian West.* Translated by Aristide Messinesi. London, 1947.

Guénon, René. *The Crisis of the Modern World.* Translated by Arthur Osborne, Marco Pallis, and Richard C. Nicholson. Ghent, NY, 2001.

————. *The Reign of Quantity and the Signs of the Times.* Translated by Lord Northbourne. Ghent, NY, 2001.

————. "The "Glorification of Work". In *Initiation and Spiritual Realization*, 54-57. Translated by Henry D. Fohr. Ghent, NY, 2001.

————. "Initiation and the Crafts". In *Miscellanea*, 57-62. Translated by H. D. Fohr. Hillsdale, NY, 2004.

————. "The Arts in Their Traditional Conception". In *Miscellanea*, 82-87. Translated by H. D. Fohr. Hillsdale, NY, 2004.

Hani, Jean. *Divine Craftsmanship: Preliminaries to a Spirituality of Work.* Translated by Robert Procter. San Raphael, CA, 2007.

Johnston, Edward. *Formal Penmanship and Other Papers.* Edited by Heather Child. London, 1971.

————. *Lessons in Formal Writing.* Edited by Heather Child and Justin Howes. London, 1986.

Johnston, Priscilla. *Edward Johnston.* Revised edition, London, 1976.

Jones, David. *Epoch and Artist*, 85-185. London, 1959.

————. "Use and Sign". In *The Dying Gaul and Other Writings*, 177-185. London, 1978.

Keeble, Brian. *Art: For Whom and For What?* Ipswich, UK, 1998.

————(ed.). *Every Man An Artist: Readings in the Traditional Philosophy of Art.* Bloomington, IN, 2005.

Leach, Bernard. "Towards a Standard". In *A Potter's Handbook*, 1-27. London, 1940.

Lethaby, W. R. *Form in Civilisation.* London, 1957.

Maritain, Jacques. *Art and Scholasticism*. Translated by J. F. Scanlan. London, 1930.

Massingham, H. J. *The Tree of Life*. London, 1943.

Messinesi, A. "A Craft as a Fountain of Grace and a Means of Realization". *Tomorrow*, Winter, 1965, Vol. 13, No. 1, 32-42.

Nasr, Seyyed Hossein. *Knowledge and the Sacred* (The Gifford Lectures, 1981). Edinburgh, 1981.

———. *Religion and the Order of Nature* (The 1994 Cadbury Lectures). New York and Oxford, 1996.

Northbourne, Lord. *Religion in the Modern World*. Ghent, NY, 2001.

Pallis, Marco, "The Active Life". In *The Way and the Mountain*. London, 1960.

Schuon, Frithjof. *Art from the Sacred to the Profane: East and West*. Edited by Catherine Schuon Bloomington, IN, 2007. (This anthology comprises selected passages, with added illustrations, from the sources listed below.)

———. "Aesthetics and Symbolism in Art and Nature". In *Spiritual Perspectives and Human Facts*, 24-49. Translated by Macleod Matheson. London, 1954.

———. "Truths and Errors Concerning Beauty". In *Logic and Transcendence*, 238-248. Translated by Peter N. Townsend. London, 1975.

———. "Foundations of an Integral Aesthetics" and "The Degrees of Art". In *Esoterism as Principle and Way*, 177-198. Translated by William Stoddart. London, 1981.

———. "Concerning Forms in Art". In *The Transcendent Unity of Religions*, 61-78. Wheaton, Ill., 1984.

———. "Art: Its Duties and Rights" and "The Spiritual Meaning of Work". In *The Transfiguration of Man*, 45-54. Bloomington, IN, 1995.

Sherrard, Philip. *The Rape of Man and Nature*. Ipswich, 1987.

———. *The Sacred in Life and Art*. Ipswich, UK, 1990.

———. *Human Image: World Image*. Ipswich, UK, 1992.

Shewring, Walter. *Making and Thinking*. London, 1956.

———. *Artist and Tradesman*. Marlborough, UK, 1984.

Sturt, George. *The Wheelwright's Shop*. Cambridge, UK, 1923.

BIOGRAPHICAL NOTES

BRIAN KEEBLE has devoted his life's work to promoting an understanding of the arts and crafts in the light of the sacred traditions. He was editor, designer, and publisher of Golgonooza Press for 30 years from 1974-2004, publishing important titles by Ananda K. Coomaraswamy, Titus Burckhardt, Eric Gill, Seyyed Hossein Nasr, Kathleen Raine, Philip Sherrard and others. He was also a founder editor of the journal *Temenos* (1980-1991) with Kathleen Raine, Philip Sherrard, and Keith Critchlow. He has published many articles and is the author of *Art: For Whom and For What?* (1998), *Conversing With Paradise* (2003), and *Every Man An Artist: Readings in the Traditional Philosophy of Art* (2005). He is a Fellow of the Temenos Academy in London, where he lectures.

WENDELL BERRY is a conservationist, farmer, essayist, novelist, professor of English, and poet. He was born in Henry Country, Kentucky, in 1934 and is the author of 32 books of essays, poetry, and novels. The *New York Times* has called Berry the "prophet of rural America". A former professor of English at the University of Kentucky and a past fellow of both the Guggenheim Foundation and the Rockefeller Foundation, Berry now lives and works on a farm near Port Royal, Kentucky. He has received numerous awards for his work, including an award from the National Institute and Academy of Arts and Letters in 1971, and the T. S. Eliot Award in 1994.

INDEX

Absolute, 77, 80, 83
abstraction, 33, 44, 61
Adam, 36, 37
aesthetics, 61, 77, 81, 88, 101
antiquarianism, 16, 23
archetype, 34; of beauty, 34, 58, 96
    archetypal Ideas, 31, 33, 36, 39
    archetypal principles, 100
    archetypal realities, 34, 98
    archetypal truths, 33
architecture, 21, 56, 83
Aristotle, 11, 45, 63
Ashbee, C. R., 2
ars, 65
artificer, 5, 7, 10, 11, 97
artist, 3, 6, 7, 9-11, 16, 17, 19, 20,
    44-46, 49, 52, 53, 55, 63-65, 68,
    70-73, 82, 86, 89, 90, 95, 96, 98
artistry, 64, 65
Arts and Crafts Movement, 3, 15, 16,
    22, 55, 56
Asclepius (Hermes), 5
Athena, 6
Augustine, St., 43
automation, 26
avant-garde, 64, 67, 70

Baroque, the, 73
beauty, 4, 9, 12, 18-20, 23, 31, 40, 43-
    46, 48, 53-58, 61-64, 73, 75, 78,
    80-83, 87, 94-96, 101-103,106,
    107; archetype of, 34, 58, 96;
    Scholastic doctrine of, 43;
    nature of, 18, 39
Being, 19, 33, 44, 61, 82, 89, 90, 92,
    95, 96
Bhagavad Gītā, 5
Blake, William, 17, 46, 47, 48, 50, 52,
    57, 85-98, 102
Boethius, 89

Bonaventure, St., 63
Buddhism, 1
Burckhardt, Titus, 25

calligraphy, 15, 30, 33, 57
Carlyle, Thomas, 46, 49, 50, 51, 52,
    53, 56
cathedrals, 23, 24, 71, 83
chaos, 90, 95
Charpentier, Louis, 25
Chiaro Oscuro, 90
Christianity, 1
Cobbett, William, 46, 48, 49, 53
Coleridge, 50, 51, 52
commodities, 26, 27
community, 3, 21
consumerism, 24, 59, 60
consumer society, 48
contemplation, 8, 30, 32, 33, 39, 40,
    81, 91, 98
Coomaraswamy, A. K., *ix, xii, xiv,*
    1-13, 16, 18, 24, 26, 41, 52, 76, 69,
    88, 102
cosmology, 4, 94, 96
crafts, 1, 2-4, 10-12, 15, 21, 23, 29,
    30, 35, 36, 47, 55, 57, 65, 83
craftsman, 3, 4, 8, 10, 11, 17, 19, 20,
    27, 29, 31, 34, 36, 37, 38, 40
craftmanship, 22, 101
Creation, 36, 37, 63, 78, 92, 93, 99,
    105
creative freedom, 70, 71, 72, 74
Creator, the, 4, 12, 36, 89, 94
Critchlow, Keith, 25
cult, 3, 57
culture, 2, 3, 10, 24, 26, 55, 64, 75

deiformity, 37, 76, 96
design, 16, 17, 20, 23, 25, 38, 58
Dionysius the Areopagite, St., 43

Diotima, 32, 33
discernment, 65, 67, 72
Divine, 4, 5, 15, 22, 24, 25, 32, 33,
    36, 37, 45, 63, 77, 78, 87, 88-90,
    92-98, 100, 102; Act, *vii*; Artist,
    94; Body, 88, 89, 92, 98; Creator,
    4; economy, 93; Image, 36, 77, 78;
    Imagination, 96; Intellect, 6, 63,
    87, 89, 94; nature, 92, 94; Oneness,
    93; Principle, 2; Providence, 15;
    Reality, 5, 98; Reason, 63; Vision,
    86, 87, 93, 95, 97; Will, 45, 97
division of labor, 3, 8, 16, 51
doctrine, 11, 24, 76, 88, 95;
    metaphysical, 59; religious, 4; of
    art, 4, 5, 7, 11, 41, 63, 72, 73, 92;
    of scientific progress, 42; of work,
    55

Earth, 32, 36, 37, 54, 60
economics, 16, 23, 26, 27, 50, 60;
economy, 19, 26, 51, 52, 60, 97, 100
Ellul, Jacques, 12
empiricism, 50
Enlightenment, the, 85, 88, 94
essence, 18, 36, 44, 45, 80, 83, 89, 91
Eternity, 86, 89, 93
expression, 18, 57, 61, 77, 90, 98
eye of the mind, 31, 32, 34

Fairbank, Alfred, 31
Faulkner, Peter, 101
fitness: of form, 23; function of, 19; of
    purpose, 19, 39; of the work, 21
free-will, 43

Genesis, 5, 36, 94
Gill, Eric, 1, 15, 16, 18, 19, 20, 21, 24,
    26, 27, 31, 34, 38, 41-62, 100, 102
goodness, 37, 38, 44, 46, 61, 75
Gorgias (Plato), 63
Grace, 5, 38
Guénon, René, 22

harmony, 36, 46, 49
Heaven, 25, 36, 86, 90, 93, 97, 101
Hephaistos, 6
Heraclitus, 32
heresy, 61
Hinduism, 1
Hobbes, Thomas, 50
Holy Bible, the, 24
holy poverty, 55
Holy Writ, 60
homo faber, 47, 81, 82
humanism, 23, 78, 98

icon, 9, 71
iconography, 85, 87, 90
imagination, 3, 7, 8, 33, 46, 68, 86
    89, 91-93, 95, 96-98
imitation, 4, 5, 6, 8, 44, 45, 58, 61, 63
immanent, 37, 77, 80, 83
industrialism, 2, 12, 47, 53, 58
industrial production, 16, 60
Infinite, 47, 59, 92, 93, 94, 95
innovation, 12, 64, 67, 70, 72, 73, 74,
    79, 100
inspiration, 6, 88, 89, 91
intellect, 4, 7, 45, 52, 61, 80, 87, 90,
    94, 95, 96
intelligence, 3, 49, 55, 57, 61, 67, 68,
    73, 77, 79, 80, 82, 86, 94
intention, 7, 44, 58, 68, 69, 86, 95
Jesus Christ, 88, 89, 94, 98
Johnston, Edward, *xii*, 15, 18, 20, 29-
    40, 46, 57, 58, 101
Johnston, Priscilla, 15, 17, 30, 35, 36,
    37, 38, 39
Jones, David, 41, 45

knowledge, 7, 11, 26, 47, 49, 67, 70,
    71, 77, 81, 85, 86, 88, 90, 91,
    94 -96, 100

labor, 2, 3, 4, 8, 9, 15-18, 23, 28, 46,
    48, 49, 51-58, 60
Lawrence, D. H., 101

Index

Lethaby, William Richard, 2, 15-28, 34, 35, 46, 56, 57, 101, 102
letterform, 15, 29, 34, 35, 39
lettering, 30, 34
Locke, John, 50
Logos, 36, 63, 89
love, 32, 51, 91; of God, *vii*

machine production, 12, 20
machinery, 9, 20, 21, 54, 60
Marx, Karl, 101
Massingham, H. J., 26
materialism, 43, 52, 85
māyā, 80
mechanical system, 47, 52, 54, 55, 58
Mediaeval Sinhalese Art (Coomaraswamy), 2, 11
metaphysical realities, 32
metaphysical transparency of phenomenal reality, 100, 103
metaphysics, *xii*; of art, 76; of Christianity, 1; of Hinduism and Buddhism, 1
microcosm, 77, 79
Middle Ages, the, 42, 56, 63
Milton, John, 94
mimesis, 6. *See also* imitation
model, 6, 51, 80; mechanical, 51
modern art, 79
modern world, *xi*, *xiii*, 10, 21, 31, 45, 46, 78, 85
modernism, 17, 23, 78
morality, 101
morals, 11, 42
Morris, William, 2, 16, 18, 20, 21, 23, 26, 46, 53, 54, 55, 56, 60, 101
mysticism, 85
myth, 22, 57, 85

naturalism, 61, 79, 82
natura naturata, 80
nature, 4, 16, 39, 44, 49, 77, 78, 80, 88, 89, 93, 94, 95, 98, 105, 107; of art, 18, 65, 70; of man, 42, 43, 45, 47, 51, 52, 58, 76, 78, 88, 92, 94, 96, 99
Nicomachean Ethics (Aristotle), 11, 45, 63
nous, 6. *See also* intellect

painting, 87, 93
paradeigma, 6
penmanship, 36, 39
perfection, *vii*, 5, 10, 13, 29, 34, 36, 43, 44, 45, 49, 50, 65, 73, 74, 102
philosophy, 3, 7, 10, 13, 23, 24, 42, 43, 50, 64, 86, 88, 89
Plato, 31, 32, 33, 34, 36, 39, 43, 45, 63, 69, 85
Plotinus, 43
poetry, 51, 86, 93, 102
prayer, *xi*, 8, 55, 86, 99
Primordial Beauty, 103
progress, 12, 42, 43
prototype, 21, 44, 63

ratio, 47, 88, 91, 92, 95
Reality, 4, 5, 91, 93, 98
reason, 7, 59, 63, 64, 66, 71, 73, 88, 91, 95
religion, 4, 5, 17, 30, 42, 51, 56, 85, 101
religio perennis, *xii*, *xiii*, 5
Renaissance, the, 64, 105
Republic (Plato), 45
Reynolds, Sir Joshua, 86, 87, 94
Ruskin, John, 2, 16, 17, 18, 23, 26, 28, 46, 49, 51, 52, 53, 54, 55, 56

sacrament, *vii*
Scholastic, 20, 24, 29, 43, 63
Schuon, Frithjof, *vii*, *xiv*, 75-83, 102
science, 9, 16, 17, 23, 50, 52, 97
sculpture, 41; erotic, 1
Self, 4, 6, 94
senses, 32, 44, 50, 77
sentimentalism, 56
sentimentality, 13, 73, 102

service, 16, 17, 18, 19, 23, 25, 56, 57

sin, 38, 45, 96; artistic, 4, 11, 96; moral, 4, 11

skill, *vii*, 10, 11, 19, 26, 27, 35, 45, 52, 57, 63, 65-74, 77

slavery, 19, 21, 60

Smith, Adam, 50

socialism, 55, 56, 58

society, 2, 4, 9, 10, 15-17, 20, 21, 25-28, 42, 48, 51, 53, 55-57, 59, 60-62, 65, 89, 97

Socrates, 32

solipsism, 82, 98

soul, 11, 32, 36, 49, 50, 52, 78, 81, 82, 88, 91, 92, 94, 98, 103

Spirit, 4, 15, 57, 79, 86, 92, 96

spiritual realities, 32, 85, 98

stonemasonry, 15

style, 16, 17, 21, 23

substance, 4, 18, 29, 34, 37, 38, 56-58, 63, 73, 77, 81-83, 87, 96

Supreme Principle, 22, 77

symbol, 6, 57; science of, 100

symbolism, 4, 21, 22, 103

Symposium (Plato), 31, 39

synergoi, 6

talent, 65, 97, 100

theomorphism of man, 78, 99, 101

Thomas, St., 4, 43, 44, 90, 91, 95

Timaeus (Plato), 69

trades, 21, 46

Trade Union, 56

tradition, 5, 35, 43, 45, 46, 56, 101

traditional doctrine of art, 24, 73, 93, 94

traditional philosophy, 10, 13; of art, 1, 3, 7, 10

transcendent, 37, 77, 80, 83

truth, 13, 35, 37, 38, 75, 80, 91, 95, 96; methapysical, 70; universal, 75

Unions, 27, 56

utility, 9, 10, 18, 19, 23, 38, 48, 50, 52, 53, 57, 60, 64

virtue, 31, 38, 39, 40, 59, 81, 82, 89

vocation, *xi*, *xii*, 1, 3, 4, 5, 11, 30, 31, 36, 40, 45, 64, 65, 75, 80, 81, 97

von Simson, Otto, 25

wealth, 16, 26, 27, 51

Whitehead, A.N., 101

wisdom, 1, 4, 5, 7, 16, 19, 26, 37, 44, 45, 48, 49, 58, 59, 63, 66, 68, 70-73, 88, 95, 97, 100-102

wood-engravings, 41

wood carvings, 41

Wordsworth, William, 86

work, *vii*, *xi*, *xii*, *xiii*, 1, 4, 7, 8, 10-12, 16-22, 24, 25, 30, 35-39, 41, 42, 44-46, 50-59, 65, 66, 70-73, 77, 78, 85, 89, 90, 95-103; as prayer, *vii*, *xi*, 8, 30, 55; industrial, 49; nature of, 49; God and, *xi*, *xii*, *xiii*, 102

worker, 3, 8, 12, 26, 48, 49, 50, 51, 54, 55, 56, 58, 67, 100

workmanship, 7, 9, 11, 18, 19, 21, 24, 26, 38, 41, 46, 47, 53, 56-58, 70, 100, 102

workshops, 3

Writing and Illuminating, and Lettering (Johnston), 15, 30, 34

Zeus, 6

For a glossary of all key foreign words used in books published by World Wisdom, including metaphysical terms in English, consult: www.DictionaryofSpiritualTerms.org. This on-line Dictionary of Spiritual Terms provides extensive definitions, examples, and related terms in other languages.

Other Titles in the Perennial Philosophy Series by World Wisdom

A Christian Pilgrim in India: The Spiritual Journey of Swami Abhishiktananda (Henri Le Saux), by Harry Oldmeadow, 2008

The Betrayal of Tradition: Essays on the Spiritual Crisis of Modernity, edited by Harry Oldmeadow, 2005

Borderlands of the Spirit: Reflections on a Sacred Science of Mind, by John Herlihy, 2005

A Buddhist Spectrum: Contributions to Buddhist-Christian Dialogue, by Marco Pallis, 2003

The Essential Ananda K. Coomaraswamy, edited by Rama P. Coomaraswamy, 2004

The Essential Martin Lings, edited by Reza Shah-Kazemi and Emma Clark, 2010

The Essential René Guénon: Metaphysics, Tradition, and the Crisis of Modernity, edited by John Herlihy, 2009

The Essential Seyyed Hossein Nasr, edited by William C. Chittick, 2007

The Essential Sophia, edited by Seyyed Hossein Nasr and Katherine O'Brien, 2006

The Essential Titus Burckhardt: Reflections on Sacred Art, Faiths, and Civilizations, edited by William Stoddart, 2003

Every Branch in Me: Essays on the Meaning of Man, edited by Barry McDonald, 2002

Every Man An Artist: Readings in the Traditional Philosophy of Art, edited by Brian Keeble, 2005

Figures of Speech or Figures of Thought? The Traditional View of Art, by Ananda K. Coomaraswamy, 2007

A Guide to Hindu Spirituality, by Arvind Sharma, 2006

Introduction to Traditional Islam, Illustrated: Foundations, Art, and Spirituality, by Jean-Louis Michon, 2008

Islam, Fundamentalism, and the Betrayal of Tradition: Essays by Western Muslim Scholars, edited by Joseph E.B. Lumbard, 2004

Journeys East: 20th Century Western Encounters with Eastern Religious Traditions, by Harry Oldmeadow, 2004

Light From the East: Eastern Wisdom for the Modern West, edited by Harry Oldmeadow, 2007

Living in Amida's Universal Vow: Essays in Shin Buddhism, edited by Alfred Bloom, 2004

Of the Land and the Spirit: The Essential Lord Northbourne on Ecology and Religion, edited by Christopher James and Joseph A. Fitzgerald, 2008

Paths to the Heart: Sufism and the Christian East, edited by James S. Cutsinger, 2002

Remembering in a World of Forgetting: Thoughts on Tradition and Postmodernism, by William Stoddart, 2008

Returning to the Essential: Selected Writings of Jean Biès, translated by Deborah Weiss-Dutilh, 2004

Science and the Myth of Progress, edited by Mehrdad M. Zarandi, 2003

Seeing God Everywhere: Essays on Nature and the Sacred,
edited by Barry McDonald, 2003

Singing the Way: Insights in Poetry and Spiritual Transformation,
by Patrick Laude, 2005

*The Spiritual Legacy of the North American Indian:
Commemorative Edition*, by Joseph E. Brown, 2007

Sufism: Love & Wisdom,
edited by Jean-Louis Michon and Roger Gaetani, 2006

*The Underlying Religion: An Introduction to the Perennial
Philosophy*, edited by Martin Lings and Clinton Minnaar, 2007

*Unveiling the Garden of Love: Mystical Symbolism in Layla
Majnun and Gita Govinda*, by Lalita Sinha, 2008

Wisdom's Journey: Living the Spirit of Islam in the Modern World,
by John Herlihy, 2009

*Ye Shall Know the Truth: Christianity and the Perennial
Philosophy*, edited by Mateus Soares de Azevedo, 2005